Treasures of the Taylorian:
Reformation Pamphlets
Volume 8

Martin Luther

Wider die Rotten der Bauern
Against the Bands of Peasants

Edited by Henrike Lähnemann and
Rahel Micklich

Taylor Institution Library, Oxford, 2025

TAYLOR INSTITUTION LIBRARY
St Giles, Oxford, OX1 3NA

http://editions.mml.ox.ac.uk

© The Authors

Some rights are reserved. This book is made available under the Creative Commons Attribution-ShareAlike 4.0 International (CC BY-SA 4.0 DEED). This licence allows for copying any part of the work for personal and non-commercial use, providing author attribution is clearly stated.

Digital downloads for this edition are available at https://editions.mml.ox.ac.uk/publications/
They include audio recording, facsimiles, and a pdf eBook of the text.

The facsimiles are of

Martin Luther, *Wider die mordischen vnd reubischen Rotten der Pawren*
 [Nuremberg: Friedrich Peypus, 1525],
 Taylorian, ARCH.8°.G.1525(27).

Martin Luther, *Wider die sturmēden Bawren.*
 Auch wider die reubischen vnd mȯrdisschen rottē der andern Bawren
 [Erfurt: Matthes Maler, 1525],
 Taylorian, ARCH.8°.G.1525(28).

The cover image is taken from ARCH.8°.G.1525(28).

Typesetting by Henrike Lähnemann
Cover design by Emma Huber

ISBN 978-1-0686058-7-1

Printed in the United Kingdom and United States by Lightning Source for Taylor Institution Library

Table of Contents

Preface	v
1. Historical Introduction (Rahel Micklich)	vii
1. The Peasants' War, or: Escalating Communication	viii
2. The Müntzer War, or: Revolutionary Faith?	xix
3. The Pamphlet War, or: Cochlaeus versus Luther	xxxii
2. The Pamphlet in the GDR (Timothy Powell)	liv
3. Peasants' War Pamphlets in Oxford (Henrike Lähnemann)	lxxiii
1. *Ermahnung zum Frieden*	lxxiii
2. *Wider die Rotten der Bauern*	lxxx
3. *Sendbrief von dem harten Büchlein wider die Bauern*	lxxxiii
4. Introduction to the Edition	lxxxvii
5. Bibliography	xc
Edition, Translation, Commentary	
Wider die Rotten der Bauern	2
Against the Bands of Peasants	3
Facsimiles of the Taylorian Copies	
Nuremberg: Friedrich Peypus, ARCH.8°.G.1525(27)	31
Erfurt: Matthes Maler, ARCH.8°.G.1525(28)	32

The Peasants' War display case in the Voltaire Room,
curated by participants of the Sommerakademie der Studienstiftung

Black letter type from the Bodleian Libraries Bibliographic Press and linocut executed by Ewa Węgrzyn based on a model by Lucas Cranach

Preface

Editing one of Martin Luther's most vicious pamphlets, *Wider die Rotten der Bauern / Against the Bands of Peasants*, has been an uncomfortable task at times. The *Sendbrief vom Dolmetschen / Open Letter on Translation*, the inaugural and fifth volume of the Taylorian Edition Series Reformation Pamphlets, promoted idiomatic use of the German language; *Von der Freiheit eines Christenmenschen / On Christian Freedom* (vol. 3), the concept of freedom; the *Mönchkalb / Monk-Calf* tempered its anti-monastic rhetoric with comedy (vol. 6); but this volume deals with a call to attack, albeit in brilliant rhetoric. The collegiality which characterised the 'band of scholars' working on this volume was a very welcome antidote to Luther's invective against the 'band of peasants'.

This volume, the eighth in the series, has grown out of a wide range of collaborations, some long-standing, others formed to publish this edition. The idea to work on a pamphlet from the Peasants' War in 1525 came from Lyndal Roper and Edmund Wareham Wanitzek, who will also be collaborating on the next volume, featuring one of the few pro-peasant pamphlets, *An die Versammlung gemeiner Bauernschaft*. The series has benefited from their expertise from its beginning: it was Edmund who introduced me to the extraordinary collection at the Taylorian with which he had been teaching students in the History Faculty. Rahel Micklich, in Oxford through a scholarship from the Humboldt Foundation, joined me on the editorial team, shouldering the burden of writing a threefold introduction which also gives voice to those opposed to Luther's vicious take on the peasants, both from the radical wing of the Reformation and from the Catholic side. Timothy Powell, who already worked on volumes 6 and 7, brought insights from his doctoral work on the reception of Hans Sachs to the chapter on *Wider die Rotten* in the GDR.

This series also aims to introduce students to historic collections and engage with digital editing. In September, Andrew Dunning, Emma Huber, Rahel Micklich and I taught an intense summer school 'Opening the Archives' for the Studienstiftung des deutschen Volkes.

The students in this group were Nico Belobrajdic, Lydia Biedermann, Paulina Bleuel, Judith Habenicht, Grace Muldowney, Benedikt Muschel, Tara Neugebauer, Laura Primavesi, Viktor Sattler, Ariane Stefanie Türk, Laura van Heijnsbergen, Jimmy Vuong, and Sarah Wieland. They produced the transcriptions, online edition, and curated a small exhibition on the topic in the Voltaire Room of the Taylorian. Their work was continued by two research interns working with me during Michaelmas Term, Tamara Klarić and Marina Giraudeau, who provided the bibliographic descriptions for all Oxford copies, continuing a great line of German students working on the Taylor Editions.

Doctoral students and colleagues helped with the edition, translation, and commentary. Ryan Hampton provided most of the historical footnotes; Howard Jones, the long-standing linguist on the Reformation pamphlet series, provided extensive help with linguistic footnotes and gave the translation the polemical punch it needed. Colin Harris helped with generous and insightful comments on the Bodleian's book-historical holdings.

As for the previous volumes, Emma Huber as the German subject librarian at the Taylor Institution and digital lead for the library provided expert help on the digital editions aspect and designed the cover. The Bodleian and Taylorian gave kind permission to reproduce images of their holdings. The photographs from the Taylorian are by Tamara Klarić; from the Bodleian by Marina Giraudeau; additional photography by Henrike Lähnemann and Rahel Micklich. Emma Huber provided the scans.

Oxford, November 2025
Henrike Lähnemann

1. Historical Introduction
Rahel Micklich

Martin Luther's *Wider die Rotten der Bauern* is "the sharpest, most controversial, and most consequential of Luther's writings on the Peasants' War".[1] The open call for ruthless violence provoked incomprehension and even rejection, not only among his opponents but also among friends and supporters. The pamphlet, however, must not be viewed in abstract, but situated and contextualised if it is to be understood in its historical and theological dimensions. The introduction is structured in the following way.

Part 1 is framed from a historical perspective. It considers the contemporary context and genesis of *Wider die Rotten*, reviews editorial features, and outlines the cultural, political, and media-related background of the work.

Part 2 is theologically oriented. It addresses 'doctrinal' differences between Luther and Müntzer against the backdrop of the escalating Peasants' War, highlighting in profile ideological conflicts that not only mirrored and shaped the course of events but also shed light on how Luther arrived at *Wider die Rotten*.

Part 3 focuses on a Bodleian copy authored by the Catholic theologian Johann Cochlaeus, containing a scathing response to Luther's text. It examines, within its historical and editorial context, the case of a media counter-reaction to Luther's *Wider die Rotten*, linking key thematic threads from Parts 1 and 2 to concrete textual instances.

---

[1] Thomas Kaufmann (2024), *Der Bauernkrieg. Ein Medienereignis*, Freiburg/Basel/Wien, 216–17 (All translations from secondary literature by R. M.). Luther communicated his final position, when he declared the situation hopeless, to his princely house, of course, also orally. Cf. Lyndal Roper (2025), *Summer of Fire and Blood. The German Peasants' War*, New York, 198.

1. The Peasants' War
or: Escalating Communication

> In the previous pamphlet, I did not venture to judge the peasants, as they had offered to take legal and further instruction, just as Christ commands us not to judge (Matthew 7). But before I even have time to look round, off they go, taking matters violently into their own hands, forgetting their offer, thieving, and running riot like mad dogs.[1]

The publication of *Wider die Rotten* was intended above all as a supplement to Luther's *Ermahnung zum Frieden*, issued only a few weeks earlier, a response to the *Zwölf Artikel* of the Upper German peasants, as is indicated by the extended title of the first edition[2], which reads: *Ermahnung zum Frieden auf die Zwölf Artikel der Bauernschaft in Schwaben. Auch wider die räuberischen und mörderischen Rotten der anderen Bauern.* That the title here speaks of the "other peasants" shows that a distinction was still made, even though the text itself then speaks of "the peasants".[3] The comparatively brief addendum to the *Ermahnungsschrift*, which was soon to lead a public life of its own, not least because Luther's opponents wished to let it 'speak for itself' (by printing it separately), indicates that the situation in the country had quickly grown more acute.

What separates the two is (*i.*) the transition of the Upper German peasant protests into violent forms of enforcing their demands, (*ii.*) their contagious spread into several central German regions, and (*iii.*) Luther's own experiences of hostility on his journey through Thuringia, where (*iv.*) he witnessed the complete failure of his attempts

---

[1] A2r; *WA* 18, 357, 3–9. Quotations from text and translation are from the new edition in this volume, with the *WA* given as parallel reference.

[2] A list of the editions, together with a stemma and linguistic characteristics, in *WA* 18, 345–56. For the Oxford copies cf. below, chapter 3.2.

[3] The 'peasantry' as it appeared in the public sphere repeatedly suggested, as in the *Zwölf Artikel 'aller' Bauernschaft* or *An die Versammlung der 'allgemeinen' Bauernschaft*, that it was acting as a collectively homogeneous 'speaking subject' ('we', 'our' …). Cf. Kaufmann (2024), 151, 184–85; also Gerd Schwerhoff (2024), *Der Bauernkrieg. Geschichte einer wilden Handlung*, München, 161.

at mediation. In the end, he was convinced that the outbreak of violence could only be met with counter-violence. His *Wider die Rotten* thus addresses the political necessity of such action, while his *Ermahnung zum Frieden* is primarily concerned with the theological legitimacy of the peasants' demands. *Wider die Rotten* is therefore less a work of controversial theology than of consequential theology: of theological politics.

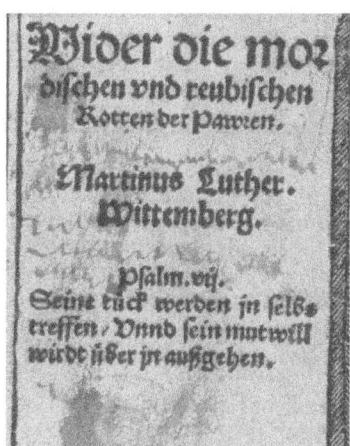 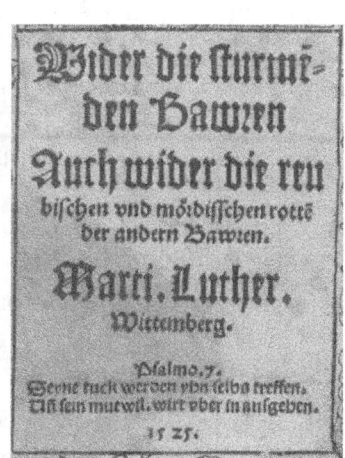

Two versions of the title in the two Taylorian copies, indicating its genesis
Nuremberg ARCH.8°.G.1525(28) / Erfurt ARCH.8°.G.1525(27)

The title of the Wittenberg first edition reads: *Ermanunge zum fride auff die zwelff artickel der Bawrschafft ynn Schwaben. Auch widder die reubischen und mȯrdisschen rotten der andern bawren.*[4] On folio E3v, at the beginning of the edition's second text *Wider die Rotten*, the heading *Widder die stürmenden bawren* is used. This title, *Wider die stürmenden Bauern*, was adopted by the Erfurt edition and combined with the main title *Wider die räuberischen und mörderischen Rotten der anderen Bauern* – unlike, for instance, the version published in Leipzig, which likewise used the title *Wider die stürmenden Bauern* but without the longer, sharper title of the Wittenberg first edition. By

---

[4] Cf. VD16 L 4692.

drawing on the original title, *Wider die stürmenden Bauern*, as it appears as heading on folio E3v, the Erfurt edition at least outwardly reflects the original publication intent of situating *Wider die Rotten* within the context of the *Ermahnungsschrift*, as the Wittenberg first edition deliberately did – although Erfurt did not reproduce the 'main' text of that publication, Luther's *Ermahnung zum Frieden*. Rather, *Wider die Rotten* was printed separately in Erfurt, as in Nuremberg and elsewhere.[5] In the Taylorian collection, both title variants are represented: the Nuremberg edition bears the title *Wider die mordischen vnd reubischen Rotten der Pawren*, while the Erfurt edition appears under *Wider die sturmenden Bawren. Auch wider die reubischen vnd mȯrdisschen rotten der andern Bawren.*

All this did not remain without consequences. In the bright light of Reformation ideas, not only did new possibilities arise for articulating experienced injustice – now recognisable to everyone as displeasing to God – but the peasants also felt encouraged to take their destiny into their own hands. It was a matter of divine justice, no longer of secular law and seigneurial arbitrariness.[6] The Gospel was to serve as the measure of all things. What was perceived, however, was a yawning gap between what the Christian faith commanded and how the authorities, both clergy and nobility, behaved, treating the peasants

---

[5] Cf. *WA* 18, 345–48.
[6] Cf. Schwerhoff (2024), 152–53, points out, in the case of the *Memminger Bundesordnung*, the *Zwölf Artikel*, and a large number of well-researched *Beschwerdeartikel* (grievance articles) from 'individual persons', 'entire communities', or 'associations of several villages', that the theological component primarily functioned as a framing device, while the content framed in this way reflected the existential interests of the peasants, including serfdom, the granting of hunting and fishing rights, the expansion of timber supplies and grazing rights, and the reduction of seigneurial burdens: "Above all, strikingly few complaints concerned religious matters in the narrow sense. [...] Nevertheless, Gey places in the foreground of his summary of the *Gravamina* the demand for the free preaching of the Word of God. [...] Schmid, as spokesperson of the peasants [and transmitter of the Baltringen peasants' grievance letters to the Swabian League], was a man so strongly shaped by the force of the new evangelical message that the emphasis on free preaching was likely important to him, even if it was not included in the majority of the grievances".

by no means as Christian brothers. Not by chance did *brotherhood* become the focal point of their orientation, even if the ideal had strict limits: it generally excluded not only 'heathens' or Catholic figures such as monks, nuns, and priests, but also women, including their wives. The rituals of brotherhood were thoroughly male.[7]

It was, of course, mainly, though not solely, representatives of the urban bourgeois intelligentsia who lent their voice to the peasantry. In Memmingen in the southwest, for example, Christoph Schappeler and Sebastian Lotzer were at the forefront: two educated townsmen, the former by training, the latter a lay theologian and political writer who came from a learned background. Lotzer is considered the principal author of the famous *Zwölf Artikel*, composed and printed probably "in the first or second week of March 1525", and regarded as authoritative throughout the period; with twenty-four editions, it became the "most influential publication of the Peasants' War".[8] One might also think of Diepold Peringer, the so-called *Bauer of Wöhrdt*, probably a former clergyman, who claimed to be unable to read or write yet gained fame as a preacher and pamphleteer. His self-fashioning as a plain, God-fearing peasant, complete with woodcut imagery recalling the Bundschuh rebels, captured the contemporary idealisation of rural virtue and the evangelical potential of the peasantry.[9]

Two principal figures, however, stand out in driving this increasingly radical discourse: Martin Luther for the princes, and Thomas Müntzer for the peasants.[10] It is not without irony that the existential

---

[7] Cf. Roper (2025), chapter 10, esp. 208–21. "Brotherhood was not apparently open to women either. Its rituals were male" (217).
[8] Kaufmann (2024), 152, 146. On the *Articles*, see generally 146–59; on their bourgeois-urban adaptation in the case of Frankfurt a. M., 159–62. With regard to Schappeler's co-authorship, Kaufmann is sceptical; cf. 400–401.
[9] Cf. Lyndal Roper (2017), *Martin Luther: Renegade and Prophet*, London, 256–58. Cf. also Kaufmann (2024), 120–23.
[10] Müntzer was, of course, not the only one to radicalise theologically: "It was not only the theology of Müntzer's that could radicalise the miners; preachers like

concerns of the peasants were less at the centre of their writing than the theological arguments used to justify or oppose uprisings against the existing order. Both were, and argued as, theologians. The climax of the discursive intensifications, to be sure, is Luther's pamphlet *Wider die Rotten der Bauern*, whose publication almost coincided with the devastating Battle of Frankenhausen (15 May 1525). But Müntzer's polemic *Hochverursachte Schutzrede und Antwort wider das geistlose, sanftlebende Fleisch zu Wittenberg* of October 1524 is likewise, alongside other texts, exemplary in its extreme rhetoric, illustrating a mode of communication that seems to preclude any compromise or mutual understanding. Müntzer's text responds to Luther's *Sendbrief an die Fürsten zu Sachsen von dem aufrührerischen Geist*, written in late summer 1524, which in turn reacted to Müntzer's provocative *Fürstenpredigt*, delivered in July 1524 at Schloss Allstedt before Elector Friedrich the Wise and his brother and later successor Johann the Steadfast, in which, creatively interpreting Dan. 2 (Nebuchadnezzar's dream of the four empires)[11], he addressed the princes with apocalyptic words, declaring that the existing social conditions and their political power structures required a profound transformation in the name of evangelical equality and brotherhood. A "bold sermon, perhaps the boldest ever heard by a ruling authority in Germany".[12]

[Georg] Amandus were developing equally powerful theologies linked to their own circumstances, and at Schneeberg, where the energetic Catholic Duke Georg was threatening to execute evangelicals while the ever-cautious Elector Friedrich counselled hearing them out, martyrdom was in the air". Roper (2025), 197.

[11] Müntzer went so far as to invent "a new version of Daniel's vision of history", which did not end with the (fourth) empire of the Romans but added yet a fifth, the Holy Roman Empire of the German Nation, an empire "that carried the depravity, hypocrisy, and ungodliness of power to its extreme, and with whose fall in the near future all empires, indeed rule itself, would collapse". "With this hint Müntzer sought to recommend himself to his princely lords as a 'new Daniel'". Cf. Hans-Jürgen Goertz (2015), *Thomas Müntzer. Revolutionär am Ende der Zeiten*, München, 145, esp. 139–51.

[12] Goertz (2015), 151. On the *Fürstenpredigt*, see esp. 133–57.

Luther's *Wider die Rotten* no longer responds to a text but to a situation. Whereas in the *Ermahnung zum Frieden*, his answer to the demands of the *Zwölf Artikel*,[13] Luther still had reconciliation in view – "the news of the peasants' atrocities had not yet reached Wittenberg"[14] – not least because the peasants themselves had expressly declared their willingness to be instructed by Scripture should their demands prove mistaken, the situation had, within a very short time, escalated dramatically. Müntzer had returned from southern Germany. In Mühlhausen, he was elected minister and, together with Heinrich Pfeiffer, overthrew the town council, installing the Eternal Council (*Ewiger Rat*) instead.[15] "Villages, castles, and monasteries were stormed, plundered, and burned by the fanatical masses", so that it was "a ghastly raging and a terrible devastation".[16] The escalation of Luther's calls for violence also had a personal reason. During his journey through Thuringia from 16 April to 6 May, Luther himself had become acquainted with the peasant movement. He preached against the uprisings and even sought to pacify the situation, "at the risk of life and limb", "threatened and mocked and filled with growing bitterness against the unbridled hordes".[17]

---

[13] At the centre is the critique of excessive corvée duties, disproportionate levies such as the tithe, inheritance taxes (the so-called *Todgeld*), and other taxes. In addition, it concerns (equal) rights of access to game, fish, poultry, and wood, since the lords controlled extensive areas of forests, waters, and airspace. These criticisms and demands appear, in one form or another, in almost all of the peasants' Articles of Complaint. Cf. Schwerhoff (2024), passim.

[14] *WA* 18, 280. To be sure, the introductions in the *Weimarer Ausgabe* (*WA*) attempted to exonerate Luther from a one-sided perspective and should therefore be treated with some caution. Kaufmann (2024, 23–53) provides an overview of the various interpretations of the Peasants' War and their scholarly tendencies.

[15] Cf. Schwerhoff (2024), 334–50.

[16] *WA* 18, 344, cf. esp. 344–45. Schwerhoff (2024, 163–350) provides a nuanced account.

[17] *WA* 18, 344. Cf. Heinz Schilling, *Martin Luther: Rebel in an Age of Upheaval*, Oxford 2017, 250: "He was confronted with demands of the southern German peasants for the first time in mid-April 1525: in the course of an inspection that ran from 13 April to 6 May [Kaufmann (2024, 200) gives 16 April as the date of departure for Eisleben],

Whereas the completion of the *Ermahnungsschrift* manuscript can be dated to before the Thuringian journey, printed in the last week of April,[18] the composition of *Wider die Rotten* took place only after Luther had witnessed the turn of events. By then, he seems to have lost all hope of reaching agreement or reconciliation, a disillusionment clearly reflected in the text. Kaufmann assumes that the drafting had already begun during the journey so that the work went to press shortly after 6 May. A letter from Hans von der Planitz to Duke Albrecht of Prussia, dated 10 May 1525, suggests that the first edition of *Wider die Rotten* was already published at that time.[19]

The pamphlet formed "the most serious reputational damage in Luther's glittering career as a virtuoso publicist".[20] Luther himself was aware of this, though he never relented in the matter, as his *Sendbrief von dem harten Büchlein wider die Bauern*, composed and published in July, after the catastrophe at Frankenhausen, with between 5,000 and 7,000 peasants killed,[21] impressively demonstrates, in which he repeated the arguments of the 'Two Kingdoms Doctrine' set out in the *Ermahnungsschrift*, which form the theological foundation for his political conclusions in *Wider die Rotten*.[22] A publication, moreover, to which he had been more or less pressed, not just to oppose the counter-reformist Emser Press in Dresden, which sought (or would seek)

---

as he travelled through the Harz forelands and into Thuringia near Weimar, he was presented with copies of the Twelve Articles and the Christian Association drawn up by the peasant assembly at Memmingen. The peasants had called upon him to adjudicate their demands, and he immediately took up that task. His verdict was published in a pamphlet entitled 'Admonition to Peace, a Reply to the Twelve Articles of the Peasants in Swabia' (*Ermahnung zum Frieden auf die zwölf Artikel der Bauernschrift in Schwaben*)".

[18] Cf. Kaufmann (2024), 409. Schilling (2017), 250, states: "This first text addressed to the peasantry was composed in Eisleben on 20 April, at some distance from the events of the uprising and at a time when news of peasant violence and plundering in Upper Swabia had not yet arrived".

[19] Cf. Kaufmann (2024), 427–28.

[20] Kaufmann (2024), 200.

[21] Cf. Schwerhoff (2024), 387.

[22] Cf. Schwerhoff (2024), 359–61.

to capitalise on Luther's uncontrolled diction,[23] but also to consolidate his own ranks,[24] since by no means all within the Wittenberg camp agreed with the tone or argumentation.[25] Yet the *Sendbrief* must be seen, together with the publication of Melanchthon's report on the *Zwölf Artikel* and his *Histori Thome Muntzers*, as part of a Wittenberg publicist counter-offensive launched in the summer of 1525 (July/August).[26]

Wider die Rotten is to be understood in the context of events; above all, however, it should be remembered that the pamphlet was published as an appendix to the much more extensive *Ermahnungsschrift* to convey that Luther had done everything in his power to defuse the situation before it escalated. Nevertheless, Luther's work appeared only twice in its original pairing with the *Ermahnung zum Frieden*: in the first edition and in a Low German version, both published in Wittenberg. All other editions, twenty-one in total, issued it separately in quarto.[27] According to Luther bibliography, *Wider die*

---

[23] The publication of *Wider die Rotten* by Luther's opponents began at the end of July 1525. They deliberately only included this pamphlet and were often accompanied by scathing glosses and rebuttals, sometimes in the form of a staged dialogue, as discussed in 1.3., with Johannes Cochlaeus as prime counter-reformist activist.

[24] "A climate of compulsive partisanship for or against him [sc. Luther] spread". Kaufmann (2024), 205.

[25] Kaufmann (2024), 200–14.

[26] Cf. Kaufmann (2024), 205. It was also about distancing himself from the radical reformers. Cf. Kenneth G. Appold, *Luther and the Peasants: Religion, Ritual, and the Revolt of 1525*, Oxford 2025, 168–75, esp. 170: "The situation in 1525 was in many ways more dire for Luther. Frederick the Wise died on May 5, calling into question the personal support he had received in 1522 and continuously thereafter. And then there were the peasants. As Luther himself frequently points out, the peasants' movement had at least the potential to upend the social and political orders of Germany. The rulers saw it as a profound threat. Luther did as well, both because, as his arguments in the antipeasant writings indicate, he sympathized with the rulers' view and also because he had been blamed for causing the rebellion. Catholic controversialists such as Jerome Emser and, more extensively, Johannes Cochlaeus took aim at Luther".

[27] Cf. Kaufmann (2024), 203.

Rotten is, in all probability, the most frequently reproduced of Luther's texts. Notably, the earliest standalone reprint (likely) originated with the anti-Reformation press run by the Dresden court theologian Hieronymus Emser, backed by the duke and aiming to exploit conflicts by reprinting provocative texts. But other presses, too, apart from Emser's, published the text as a separate edition: Dresden and Erfurt (three each), Leipzig (two), Hagenau, Mainz, Würzburg, and Augsburg (two each), Landshut, Tübingen, and Nuremberg (two each), Bamberg, Regensburg, and Strasbourg (two each). It was hardly coincidental that Wittenberg, "the most productive Reformation printing centre of the time", did not take part in this publishing offensive.[28] At the same time, "the separation of the two texts and the resulting decontextualisation by his opponents scarcely absolve Luther from the accusation of undue harshness, since he himself could, after all, claim a certain copyright for the practice of furnishing opponents' texts with commentary".[29] However, the fact that the pamphlet appeared contemporaneously with the Battle of Frankenhausen "implies two points: (*i.*) that Luther, with his text, did not provide any final impulse for the military action of the princely coalition, and (*ii.*) that the cruel exhortations contained in it, 'to stab, strike, and strangle, whoever can',[30] could nonetheless, in the public perception, be held responsible *ex post* for that very massacre".[31]

The main arguments of the text, which appeared in more than twenty editions and several counter-publications, revolve around three central points: (*i.*) the faithless breach of the commandment to obey the authority ordained by God; (*ii.*) the subversion, indeed destruction, of the natural order of creation and preservation; and (*iii.*) the diabolical misuse of the Gospel as a source of justification for self-

---

[28] Cf. Kaufmann (2024), 204.
[29] Schwerhoff (2024), 358–59. Cf. Thomas Kaufmann, *Die Mitte der Reformation*, Tübingen 2019, 162–63.
[30] A4r; *WA* 18, 361, 25.
[31] Cf. Kaufmann (2024), 201.

willed action. The latter point constitutes for Luther the decisive affront, the rejection of which already ran as a theme through his earlier *Ermahnungsschrift* and now again in *Wider die Rotten*. "Even though in *Wider die stürmenden Bauern*, in view of the concrete situation of rebellious peasants, Luther spoke 'differently' with regard to the behaviour expected of the authorities than he had done in the *Ermahnung zum Frieden* [...], the politico-theoretical and theological foundations of his argumentation had not changed."[32]

In the Nuremberg copy of *Wider die mordischen und reubischen Rotten der Pawren* held in the Taylorian Library, which forms the basis of our edition, whose provenance is unknown, two brief contemporary marginal notes can be found, offering a rather dry, or perhaps ironic, commentary on Luther's verbal vehemence.

ARCH.80.G.1525(27), A2r, *gemachh* as marginal comment

ARCH.80.G.1525(27), A4r, *seüberlich* as marginal comment

The drastic "Drumb soll hie zuschmeissen / wurgen vnd stechen / heymlich / oder offenlich / wer da kan"[33] ("So, in this situation, whoever can do so should smash, throttle, and stab them, in secret or in the open") is accompanied by a succinct "gemachh" ("slowly!"), while a laconic "seüberlich" ("neatly", "sound") appears at the end beside

---

[32] Kaufmann (2024), 203.
[33] A2r; *WA* 18, 358, 14–15.

the exhortation *Drumb lieben Herren loset hie / rettet hie / helfft hie / erbarmet euch der armen leut / Steche / schlahe / würge hie wer da kan / bleybstu drüber todt / wol dir / seliglichern tod kanstu nymmer mehr überkomen. Denn du stirbst in gehorsam Göttlichs wortes vnd befelhs*[34] ("And so, dear lords, come and redeem, come and rescue, come and help, have mercy on these poor folk! Whoever can do so, come and stab, strike, and strangle! If you die in doing so, good for you: a more blessed death you can never achieve, for you die in obedience to God's word and commandment"). Both annotations are insignificant in terms of content (though nonetheless worth noting)[35] and do not appear to be by the same hand, although this cannot be entirely ruled out. Were the social setting of the marginalia known – for instance, as in the case of the Erfurt copy held by the Taylorian Library, which belonged to the Cistercians in Salem – then an ironic or even cynical reading would not be out of the question. Taking the marginal notes at face value, the following emerges. While the first, which comments with *gemachh*, occurs at a point where Luther, rhetorically overwrought, calls for open violence, the other, also placed beside a passage inciting such violence, adds *seüberlich*. Both notes, therefore, would appear not to come from opponents but from readers who more or less agreed with Luther: the first hand with some reservation, the second with open approval. The first annotation thus seems to come from someone who viewed at least the rhetorical excess critically, while the second appears to stem from a reader who regarded both the substance of what was said and its expression as justified.

---

[34] A4r; *WA* 18, 361, 24–28.
[35] Their value, of course, lies in shedding light on contemporary reader reception.

2. The Müntzer War or: Revolutionary Faith?

> He seeks to abolish Scripture and the spoken Word of God, to eradicate the sacraments of baptism and the altar, and to lead us into the spirit, where we are to tempt God with our own works and free will, waiting upon His action while prescribing to Him time, place, and measure if He should wish to act with us.[1]

Luther's struggle against the clerical power of Rome was a *theological* struggle. It was not a *political* one, even though it had political consequences. The same applies to his conflict with the peasants. What he opposed was more their abuse of the Gospel than their uprising as such. In his *Ermahnung zum Frieden*, he concedes to the peasants the right to appeal to nature, to natural law (*naturlich recht*), in order to protest injustice, but by no means to the name of Christ (*Christus namen mit friden lassen*) and to Christian 'law' (*Christlich recht*).[2] "Therefore the peasants ought rightly let the name of Christian alone, and act in some other name, as men who want human and natural rights (*menschlich und naturlich recht*), not as those who seek Christian rights (*Christlich recht*). This means that on all these points they should keep still, suffer, and make their complaints to God alone".[3] Luther's treatise *On The Freedom of a Christian* ("Von der Freiheit eines Christenmenschen"), published in 1520,[4] which was open to a radical interpretation, makes clear what mattered to him. It begins with the decisive double thesis, referencing 1 Cor. 9:19:

---

[1] *WA* 15 (*Ein Brief an die Fürsten zu Sachsen von dem aufrührerischen Geist*), 216, 29 – 217, 2. [Transl. R. M.]

[2] *WA* 18, 316, 1–4, 319, 9–14. Cf. *Wider die Rotten*, *WA* 18, 358, 19–23: "In doing this they become the greatest ever blasphemers of God and slanderers of his holy name and so honour and serve the devil under the pretence of the Gospel". (A2r)

[3] *WA* 18, 328, 4–8. (Transl. C. M. Jacobs)

[4] Although Luther's *Freiheitsschrift* outwardly appears to respond to the papal bull of excommunication *Exsurge Domine* (15 June 1520), "with this tract Luther did not react to specific controversial-theological confrontations or questions imposed upon him", but rather pursued "his own agenda", his "very own inclinations and interests". Cf. Kaufmann (2019), 632, esp. 628–46. Luther, Melanchthon, and the papal envoy Karl von Miltitz, who had not yet abandoned his diplomatic hopes of mediation,

On the one hand: "A Christian is a free lord over all things and subject to no one".
On the other hand: "A Christian is a bound servant of all things and subject to everyone".[5]

This is only seemingly a paradox. For the (negative) freedom *from* the world of sin, which Christ has wrought, is, precisely because one has been freed from it, a (positive) freedom *for* the world. Only by escaping the bonds of this world can one freely bind oneself to it. Christian freedom thus makes possible a *new relationship* to the world. Luther understands this relationship, with Paul, as *service* to the world. It is not the world that changes, but the Christian's relation to it. The price of this victory over the world is the cross within the world. For love in a loveless world means suffering. Righteousness here is not cheap but costly, as it says in Luke 9:23: "If any man will come after me, let him deny himself, and take up his cross daily, and follow me." (KJV) The reality of Christian freedom is therefore love, which is long-suffering and kind, which "envieth not", "vaunteth not itself", "is not puffed up", "beareth all things", and "endureth all things", as stated in the First Epistle to the Corinthians (1 Cor 13:4–7).

The theological mastermind *par excellence* to justify the peasant uprisings was, without doubt, Thomas Müntzer, who interpreted Luther's idea of 'Christian freedom for the world as service to the world' not as 'passion' (*passio*) but as action (*actio*). Müntzer wanted more than the Reformation of the Church; he wanted to reform the Reformation. He understood Luther's 'priesthood of all believers' to mean that before God all people are equal, an equality no longer confined

---

agreed on 12 October 1520 to backdate the conciliatory dedicatory letter prefixed to the Latin edition to 6 September, in order to create the impression that the treatise had been written before the appearance of the bull at Meissen on 21 September. It was therefore composed after 12 October and went to press in Wittenberg in November. "The entire textual compilation will have been completed in manuscript form by late October or early November" (ibid. 638). (All translations from secondary literature by R. M.)

[5] Transl. https://editions.mml.ox.ac.uk/editions/freiheit-1520/, A2v.

to the spiritual,[6] but claiming worldly reality. The *reform of the Church* must therefore be followed by a *reform of society*. From at least 1524 onwards, since his *Fürstenpredigt*, Müntzer aimed at the abolition of the estate-based social order. God, he proclaimed, promised all people equality, freedom, and brotherhood, not only in heaven, but already here on earth. Against the backdrop of a situation seen as increasingly unjust, this touched a highly sensitive and easily inflamed nerve among the peasants. Luther could find nothing in this to commend. The conflict between the two may be understood as that between a *theology of Reformation* and a *theology of Revolution*[7], or, as one might say today, a 'theology of liberation'.[8] God, according to

---

[6] Luther conceived of the freedom of a Christian likewise as spiritual, yet bound to the Word of Scripture. Christian freedom is gained as the assurance of forgiveness bestowed by grace. This concerns both its 'negative' aspect, liberation *from* the bonds of the world, and its 'positive' aspect, the ability, on this basis, to turn anew toward the world, now, however, under the 'logic' of the Gospel, that is, the 'law' of the Kingdom of God. Kaufmann speaks of a "problematic model of dichotomous anthropology", which (too sharply) accentuates "the distinctness and independence of the bodily and the spiritual nature of the Christian". Cf. Kaufmann (2019), 642. The problem continues later in the theological endeavour to define the concept of faith more precisely between (forensic) 'Gerechtsprechung' (*pronuntiari seu reputari*) and 'Gerechtwerdung' (*effici seu regenerari*). Cf. F. Nüssel, *Allein aus Glauben. Zur Entwicklung der Rechtfertigungslehre in der konkordistischen und frühen nachkonkordistischen Theologie*, Göttingen 2000, 31–61. The move away from an emphasis on effective 'Gerechtwerdung' (becoming righteous), which, after all, underlies the concept of 'Gerechtmachung' (making righteous), was not coincidentally related to the experiences with the so-called *Schwärmer*, with Anabaptists (Balthasar Hubmaier, Hans Denck, Hans Hut, Pilgram Marpeck, etc.), but especially with Müntzer. On the problem of the Anabaptists as an essential aspect of the Radical Reformation, cf. Th. Kaufmann, *Die Täufer. Von der radikalen Reformation zu den Baptisten*, München 2019b; Hans-Jürgen Goertz (1980), *Die Täufer. Geschichte und Deutung*, München.

[7] Goertz (2015), 236.

[8] The question of power had become universalised, as Roper (2025), 124, notes with regard to the radical pamphlet *An die Versammlung der gemeinen Bauernschaft* from early May 1525, an anonymous reflection from the southwest of the Empire in the spirit of Müntzer of the *Twelve Articles* and the *Memmingen Federal Ordinance*, but probably also of Luther's *Ermahnung zum Frieden* (cf. Kaufmann 2024, 183–92): "This pamphlet is the fullest attempt to provide a theology that justifies revolt and explains what is meant by 'wanting to have no lords'".

Müntzer, would wrest the sword from the unjust rulers and place it into the hands of the common people. In this spirit[9], the peasants' open revolt broke out, first in southern Germany, in Upper Swabia, the Allgäu, and Franconia, later also in central Germany, in Saxony, Thuringia, and the Harz. Monasteries were plundered.[10] Nights were spent carousing in cellars bursting with provisions. People took back what, as they said, rightfully belonged to them.[11] Later, castles too were targeted, once the rebels had acquired artillery.[12] There was iconoclasm. Figures of saints and relics were regarded as the detested expressions of idolatry and wastefulness.[13] The Marxist Günter Vogler aptly sums up in his book on the Peasants' War: "The most striking consequence was that the actions were no longer directed solely against ecclesiastical feudalism, although bishops, abbots, priests, and monks continued to be fiercely attacked, but that the assault now extended also to the secular feudal powers, thereby bursting the Reformation framework of the revolutionary movement."[14] While Müntzer and several of the peasant leaders, who themselves

---

[9] Meant is cultural disposition, which then requires a triggering factor. The concrete occasions and aims could vary greatly. Cf. Schwerhoff (2024), 541–46, who notes that suggestively composed overarching depictions following a cumulative logic no longer argue with precision, as when "situational utterances by hate-filled actors calling for the death of all priests and nobles are blown up into programmatic visions of an egalitarian society" (ibid., 542).

[10] Cf. Louisa Bergold, Charlotte Gauthier, Lyndal Roper, Edmund Wareham Wanitzek, *Visualising the Destruction of Convents and Monasteries in the German Peasants' War*, https://germanpeasantswar.web.ox.ac.uk/ (11 November 2025).

[11] "The demands and aims of the insurgents were initially expressed in numerous *gravamina* and series of articles, which primarily called for the abolition of specific abuses". Schwerhoff (2024), 541. As a rule, acts of violence occurred only later, especially in the spring of 1525. Cf. also Roper (2025), chapter 7. They were often motivated by the need to secure provisions and everyday necessities for the peasant bands.

[12] Cf., for example, Schwerhoff (2024), 238: "[…] the entire noble way of life was fundamentally called into question. […] the path was lined not only with plundered and destroyed monasteries, but also with noble residences engulfed in flames".

[13] The events, which repeated themselves everywhere, are traced in almost full geographical coverage by Schwerhoff (2024) and Roper (2025).

[14] Günter Vogler (³1983), *Die Gewalt soll gegeben werden dem gemeinen Volk. Der deutsche Bauernkrieg 1525*, Berlin, 43.

were not peasants, questioned all authority, Luther questioned only the clergy, believing it was corrupting the Church under the guise of priesthood. However, "Martin Luther and his followers had already called into question fundamental elements of the social order of the time". This concerned the dissolution of the papal church, the abolition of the clergy and of canon law; monasteries and religious orders were challenged, as was church property.[15] This became the decisive accusation made by Emser and Cochlaeus against Luther: that he was a hypocrite, having himself invoked the spirit of violence.[16]

Müntzer did not oppose *per se* the famous 13th chapter of Paul's Epistle to the Romans, which states that one should be subject to authority, for all authority comes from God, and whoever resists the ruling power resists God's command (Rom. 13:1–2). According to Müntzer and several of the peasants' Articles (notably the *Schwarzwälder Artikelbrief* and the *Sendbrief an die Versammlung der gemeinen Bauernschaft*), however, authority must behave in a Christian way. For Luther, this amounts to a categorial error, as it conflates the secular with the Church. Rather, a distinction must be made between the *realm of the world*, governed by natural law (*ius naturae, lex naturalis*), which is the order of creation and preservation, and the *realm of God*, in which love rules, and thus service to one another. The principle of love, which exists only in the (true) Church, cannot be imposed upon the world, nor expected of it. Christians endure and suffer injustice.

---

[15] Schwerhoff (2024), 581–82. On the problem of the Reformation's impact on monasteries and convents, the resistance of those affected, and the (sometimes) compromise-oriented success of negotiations, cf. Henrike Lähnemann and Eva Schlotheuber, *The Life of Nuns: Love, Politics, and Religion in Medieval German Convents*, Cambridge 2024, in particular chapter 6, 'Reformation' (127–53). See also Henrike Lähnemann (2016), 'Der Medinger 'Nonnenkrieg' aus der Perspektive der Klosterreform: Geistliche Selbstbehauptung 1479–1554', in *1517–1545: The Northern Experience. Mysticism, Art and Devotion between Late Medieval and Early Modern. Antwerp Conference 2011*, ed. Kees Scheepers et al., *Ons Geestelijk Erf* 87, 91–116.

[16] Cf. the discussion of Johann Cochlaeus in the next chapter.

They live the Kingdom of God *in* the world, without the world being the Kingdom of God. "For baptism does not make person and property free, but the soul."[17] Conversely, authority, even Christian authority, does not have the task of loving, but of preserving the existing order, even if it requires the sword.[18] In this view, the sign of the Church is love, which manifests itself in the world outside the Church as passive, suffering righteousness. To endure the cross, not to inflict the cross, is Luther's maxim, as he makes clear in his *Ermahnungsschrift*, where he states: "And that you, too, may know that you are fighting the rulers not as Christians but as heathen. For Christians fight for themselves not with sword and gun, but with the Cross and with suffering."[19] Therefore, it is and can only be: "Suffering, suffering; cross, cross! This and nothing else, is the Christian law (*Christen recht*)!"[20] Luther's primary reproach of the insurgents is not that they revolt, which is reprehensible anyway. What he criticises is the misuse of the Gospel, the misuse of the name of Christ, hence the misuse of the Word of God:

> Therefore I say again, however good and right your cause may be, nevertheless, because you would defend yourselves, and suffer neither violence nor wrong, you may do anything that God does not prevent [within the framework of Creation], but leave the name of Christian out of it; leave out, I say, the name of Christian, and do not make it a

---

[17] A2v; *WA* 18, 359, 4–5. It is striking that here, in *Wider die Rotten*, it is no longer the Christian service and suffering for the world and in the world that is emphasised, as it formed the main tenor of the *Ermahnungsschrift*, but rather the harsh consequences of disobedience that take centre stage.

[18] Cf. *Sendbrief von dem harten Büchlein wider die Bauern*, *WA* 18, 389, 14–24: "There are two kingdoms, one the kingdom of God, the other the kingdom of the world. […] God's kingdom is a kingdom of grace and mercy, not of wrath and punishment. In it there is only forgiveness, consideration for one another, love, service, the doing of good, peace, joy, etc. But the kingdom of the world is a kingdom of wrath and severity. In it there is only punishment, repression, judgment, and condemnation, for the suppressing of the wicked and the protection of the righteous (*die fromen*)". (Transl. C. M. Jacobs, slightly revised R. M.)

[19] *WA* 18, 315, 10–13. (Transl. C. M. Jacobs)

[20] *WA* 18, 310, 10–11. (Transl. C. M. Jacobs)

cloak (*schanddeckel*) for your impatient, unpeaceful, unchristian undertaking. I will neither leave it to you nor grant it to you; with writings and words I will wrest it from you (*euch abreyssen*), as far as I am able and as long as a vein in my body still beats.[21]

For Müntzer, to endure injustice was no option. Müntzer sought the universal Church. He did not aim at ecclesial democracy, but at political theocracy. The Church was to become the visible Church, not a Church *in* the world, but the Church of the world. This made the upheaval of the existing conditions necessary. Hans-Jürgen Goertz notes: "By depriving secular authority of its basis of legitimacy, […], Müntzer shattered the right of rule and replaced it with the right of the (parish) community, in which everyone is ready to serve everyone."[22] Accordingly, "rule […] will fall to the people, who have reintegrated themselves into the divine order, the original relationship to God [*ante lapsum!*]".[23] Müntzer's claim is therefore to overcome sin, indeed to establish the Kingdom of God here and now. "He wished to make way for the arrival of the divine kingdom on earth."[24]

The theological conflict between Luther and Müntzer[25] concerned the latter's radical reading of Luther's *sola fide* and 'universal priesthood'. Müntzer spiritualised the individual's relationship with God more 'deeply' than Luther, for whom it bore above all ecclesiological implications (*ecclesia enim nascitur verbo promissionis per fidem*)[26], setting it against a priesthood that stood between God and man (as

---

[21] *WA* 18, 314, 9–17. (Transl. C. M. Jacobs, partially revised R. M.)
[22] Goertz (2015), 235.
[23] Goertz (2015), 232.
[24] Goertz (2015), 226.
[25] On Müntzer as a theologian, cf. the collected volume ed. by Siegfried Bräuer and Helmar Junghans (1989), *Der Theologe Thomas Müntzer. Untersuchungen zu seiner Entwicklung und Lehre*, Berlin, in particular Martin Brecht, 'Thomas Müntzers Christologie', 62–83; Hans-Jürgen Goertz, 'Zu Thomas Müntzers Geistverständnis', 84–99; Eric W. Gritsch, 'Thomas Müntzers Glaubensverständnis', 156–73; Eike Wolgast, 'Die Obrigkeits- und Widerstandslehre Thomas Müntzers'; and Reinhard Schwarz, 'Thomas Müntzer und die Mystik', 283–301.
[26] *WA* 6 (= *De captivitate Babylonica ecclesiae*, 1520), 560, 33–34.

"gatekeepers for the eternal salvation of all believers")[27], which is why now all who believe, by virtue of their relationship with God, are priests (*nos omnes esse aequaliter sacerdotes*)[28]. Luther's *sola scriptura* principle was thereby undermined, or at least devalued. The claim was no longer that God pronounces the individual righteous extrinsically, that is, passively (in terms of Christ's *iustitia aliena*)[29], but that one's relationship with God effects a *real* transformation, almost an intrinsic 'transsubstantiation', thus overriding Luther's *simul iustus et peccator*. Luther's theology of justification was christologically grounded; Müntzer's pneumatologically.[30] As Hans-Jürgen Goertz explains: "Faith drawn from Scripture alone, Müntzer maintained, is false, for Scripture merely bears witness to the path to faith, but not to faith itself." Rather, it concerns a "faith flowing from instruction by the divine Spirit in the 'abyss of the soul' and from the Word, which from within allows one to understand Scripture and affirms it. […] It is not in *sola scriptura*, but in the immediate working of the divine Spirit that the reformational character of divine grace is manifested."[31] Müntzer's apocalyptic conceptions therefore simultaneously betray a mystical background.[32] The inner purification of the soul, which redefines the individual's relationship to the world,[33] pre-

---

[27] Schwerhoff (2024), 28.

[28] *WA* 6, 564, 6; ibid., 566, 26–27: *Esto itaque certus et sese agnoscat quicunque se Christianum esse cognoverit, omnes nos aequaliter esse sacerdotes.*

[29] Romans 3:28: *Arbitramur enim iustificari hominem per fidem sine operibus legis.* ("We thus conclude that a man is justified by faith without the deeds of the law". KJV)

[30] "As the conflict progressed, it became increasingly clear that pneumatology, the revelation of the divine Spirit in humanity, became the defining feature of Müntzer's theology". Goertz (2015), 67.

[31] Goertz (2015), 165–66.

[32] Cf. Goertz (2015), 144.

[33] The relationship to the world that arises from the God-relationship reconstituting the human interior means more than for Luther, for whom the world does not change together with the self: "The external orders are not objectively given entities; they have no ontologically grounded status, but are the result of the relations that

cedes acting in the world – indeed is its condition: "Just as the dominion of sin within the human heart must be broken, so too must dominion in the external world, which has sprung from sinful inwardness, be destroyed, in order to bring about the breakthrough of the realm in which God's Spirit is poured out upon all flesh (Joel 2)."[34]

Luther and Müntzer represent irreconcilable concepts of the Reformation within the 'shared' space of the Reformation. For both, faith was passively grounded in the Word of God (God being the subject); yet in Luther's case, this occurred via Holy Scripture as the extrinsic event of a forensic justification (*fides imputativa*), upon which the certainty of one's faith could be built,[35] whereas in Müntzer's case it was the effective event of an inner speaking (*fides efficax*),[36] which one

---

humans enter into [...]". Goertz (2015), 147. Müntzer seems to withdraw all normative substantiality from the world and assign it to faith, so that the (faithful) subject becomes the centre of his thought.

[34] Goertz (2015), 146.

[35] In faith, the Christian receives Christ's righteousness; Christ takes upon Himself the sins of the justified. In faith, man fulfils the commandments and shares in Christ's kingly and priestly rule. The 'general priesthood of Christians' consists in being 'exalted by faith so far above all things as to become spiritually lords of all, for nothing can imperil their salvation. Indeed, everything must be subject to them and work towards their salvation'". (*ubir alle ding, das er aller eyn herr wirt geystlich, denn es kan yhm kein ding nit schaden zur seligkeit. Ja es muß yhm alles unterthan seyn und helffen zur seligkeyt*). By virtue of the general priesthood, Christians intercede for one another". Kaufmann (2019), 643 (quotation = WA 7, 27, 22–24; https://editions.mml.ox.ac.uk/editions/freiheit-1520/).

[36] That this (crucial) difference gradually emerged within the Lutheran camp, particularly in response to misleading interpretations of justification, esp. in connection with the *Augsburg Confession* and its various *Apologies*, and under the intellectual leadership of Melanchthon, is demonstrated by Nüssel (2000), 31–48, in comparison with Luther, 48–61. Luther's own semantics left scope for more effectual readings of 'faith.' Not untypical are, for example, the following words from his *Freiheitsschrift*, WA 7, 24, 33–35: "Only the word and faith reign in the soul. Through the word, the soul becomes like the word, just as iron becomes red-hot by its union with fire". (https://editions.mml.ox.ac.uk/editions/freiheit-1520/) A hermeneutics of divine *furor* is at least in the air. One is dealing with Luther's motif of the 'joyous exchange' (*commercium admirabile*). Cf. Anja Ghiselli, Kari Kopperi, and Rainer Vinke (eds.)

was obliged to obey, so that the experienced passivity (*experientia fidei*)[37] was to pass into an activity derived therefrom.[38] Luther's *Romans lecture* of 1515/16 almost seems to anticipate what he might have answered in response to Müntzer's claims:

> Those who are sanctified are, in themselves, always sinners; therefore, they are always justified from outside themselves. Hypocrites, on the other hand, are inwardly always righteous; therefore, they are always sinners from outside themselves. I say *inwardly*, that is, how we are in ourselves, in our own eyes, in our own estimation; and *outwardly*, (that is), how we are before God and in his reckoning. Therefore, we are justified from outside when we are not righteous in ourselves or by our own works, but by God's reckoning alone. For his reckoning does not belong to us, nor is it in our power. Therefore, our righteousness is neither part of us nor in our power.[39]

(1993), *Luther und Ontologie. Das Sein im Glauben als strukturierendes Prinzip der Theologie Luthers*, Helsinki/Erlangen, esp. 9–27 and 28–34. By 1540, Luther understood Christian existence *coram Deo* unequivocally in an imputative-relational sense: *Christianus est dupliciter considerandus, in praedicamento relationis et qualitatis. Si consideratur in relatione, tam sanctus est [...], id est, imputatione per Christum, quia Deus dicit, se non videre peccatum propter filium suum unigenitum [...]. Sed christianus consideratus in qualitate est plenus peccato*". WA 39/II, 142, 1–6. For the discussion of "what kind of reality then belongs to a 'relational having' (157), cf. Berthold Wald (2015), *Luthers Theologie und Anthropologie im Spiegel seiner Biographie*, Aachen, 145–63, esp. 157–63.

[37] "Müntzer, by contrast, relies on the *experientia fidei*, the experience of faith, in which the authority of God is perceived directly and without the mediation of Scripture as the basis of salvation". Goertz (2015), 66.

[38] Just as Luther, in his *Freedom of a Christian*, defended evangelical freedom against the priestly Church, which obstructed the individual's relationship with God by positioning itself as a sacramental mediator between God and the believer, so Müntzer casts Luther in a comparable role: that of one who stands in the way of God by placing the principle of Scripture above the principle of the Spirit.

[39] [Transl. R. M.] WA 56, 268, 27 – 269, 4 (commenting on Rom 4:7): *Sancti intrinsece sunt peccatores semper, ideo extrinsece iustificantur semper. Hipocrite autem intrinsece sunt iusti semper, ideo extrinsece sunt peccatores semper. Intrinsece dico, i. e. quomodo in nobis, in nostris oculis, in nostra estimatione sumus, extrinsece autem, quomodo apud Deum et in*

In his *Ermahnungsschrift* Luther still warned, above all with Müntzer in mind, "Therefore, dear brethren, I beg you, in a kindly and brotherly way, to look diligently to what you do, and not to believe all kinds of spirits and preachers, now that Satan has raised up many evil spirits of disorder and of murder (*rotten geyster und mordgeyster*), and filled the world with them."[40] He also expressed his hope that some agreement might still be possible: "Listen, then, and allow yourselves to be told something, as you have indeed offered repeatedly."[41] Yet in *Wider die Rotten* his patience is exhausted and all hope gone. Not only are 'the peasants' (*die bawrn*) exposed as "faithless, perjured, disobedient, rebellious murderers, robbers, blasphemers",[42] but the authorities are said to have the natural duty, even if they were pagan,[43] namely "the right and authority" (*recht und macht*), to punish such behaviour.[44] Luther goes one step further, arguing that this must be done even through "murder or bloodshed" (*durch mord odder blutvergiessen*), and that failing to do so is a sin against God.[45] The climax of his rhetorical derailment, however, lies in his conclusion that those who die on the side of the authorities fall as martyrs, indeed that one could earn heaven through such bloodshed (!). It had come to such a point, he claims, because of the enemies of law and order, so that "a prince can earn his place in heaven by shedding blood better than others can by praying."[46] It should, however, be noted that Luther still includes one proviso, namely that it was not enough to secure

---

reputatione eius sumus. Igitur extrinsece sumus iusti, quando non ex nobis nec ex operibus, sed ex sola Dei reputatione iusti sumus. Reputatio enim eius non in nobis nec in potestate nostra est. Ergo nec iustitia nostra in nobis est nec in potestate nostra.

[40] *WA* 18, 301, 1–4. (Transl. C. M. Jacobs)
[41] *WA* 18, 301, 4–5. (Transl. R. M.)
[42] A3r; *WA* 18, 359, 22–23.
[43] A3r; *WA* 18, 359, 20: "ob sie gleich das Euangelion nicht leydet" ("even those rulers who do not accept the Gospel").
[44] A3r; *WA* 18, 359, 23–25.
[45] Cf. *WA* 18, 360, 1–11, ibid. 5–7: "For if he can punish and does not do so, even if by murder or bloodshed, he is guilty of all the murder and evil that these scoundrels commit". (A3r).
[46] A4r; *WA* 18, 361, 4–6.

external justice – what counted was the inner motivation for doing so: "But rulers have a clear conscience (*gut gewissen*) and a just cause and can say to God with all certainty in their hearts (*mit aller sicherheyt des hertzens*): 'Look, my God, you have appointed me as a prince or a lord – of this I can have no doubt (*nicht kan zweyffeln*) – and you have entrusted me with the sword to wield over evildoers."[47] The inward certainty of one's heart, firmly rooted in faith, thus constitutes the prerequisite for 'earning' heaven.[48] In this respect, the additional condition holds that, *because* one believes, one acts accordingly, in this case: kills and slays one's enemies. Hence Pagan rulers, for example, could by no means 'earn' salvation through such deeds.[49]

Luther's *Wider die Rotten* is, after all, far more intricate than it appears at first sight, as the historical and theological background outlined above has likely made clear. And yet, its rhetorical surface operates through deliberate reduction, seeking the incisive formula, its sole aim being to produce the effect the author deems necessary. Thus, Luther's response to Müntzer's radical Reformation is unmistakable, and therefore unequivocal: "And so, dear lords, come and redeem, come and rescue, come and help, have mercy on these poor folk! Whoever can do so, come and stab, strike, and strangle! If you die in doing so, good for you: a more blessed death you can never achieve."[50]

---

[47] A3v; *WA* 18, 360, 15–18.
[48] Cf. *Sendbrief von dem harten Büchlein wider die Bauern*, *WA* 18, 398, 3–8: "For I die in rightful service to God, insofar as the deed itself is concerned. But if faith were added, I would be a true and holy martyr of God". (Transl. R. M.) Cf. ibid., *WA* 18, 399, 38 – 400, 1: "And yet it remains true that deeds count for nothing before God; only faith matters". (Transl. R. M.)
[49] And one may further ask how it then stands with the 'false believers' of the Catholic Counter-Reformation, for example with the Albertine Duke of Saxony, George the Bearded, with whom the Ernestine Electorate of his cousin Frederick the Wise effectively cooperated in order to suppress the peasant uprising in central Germany.
[50] A4r; *WA* 18, 361, 24–26.

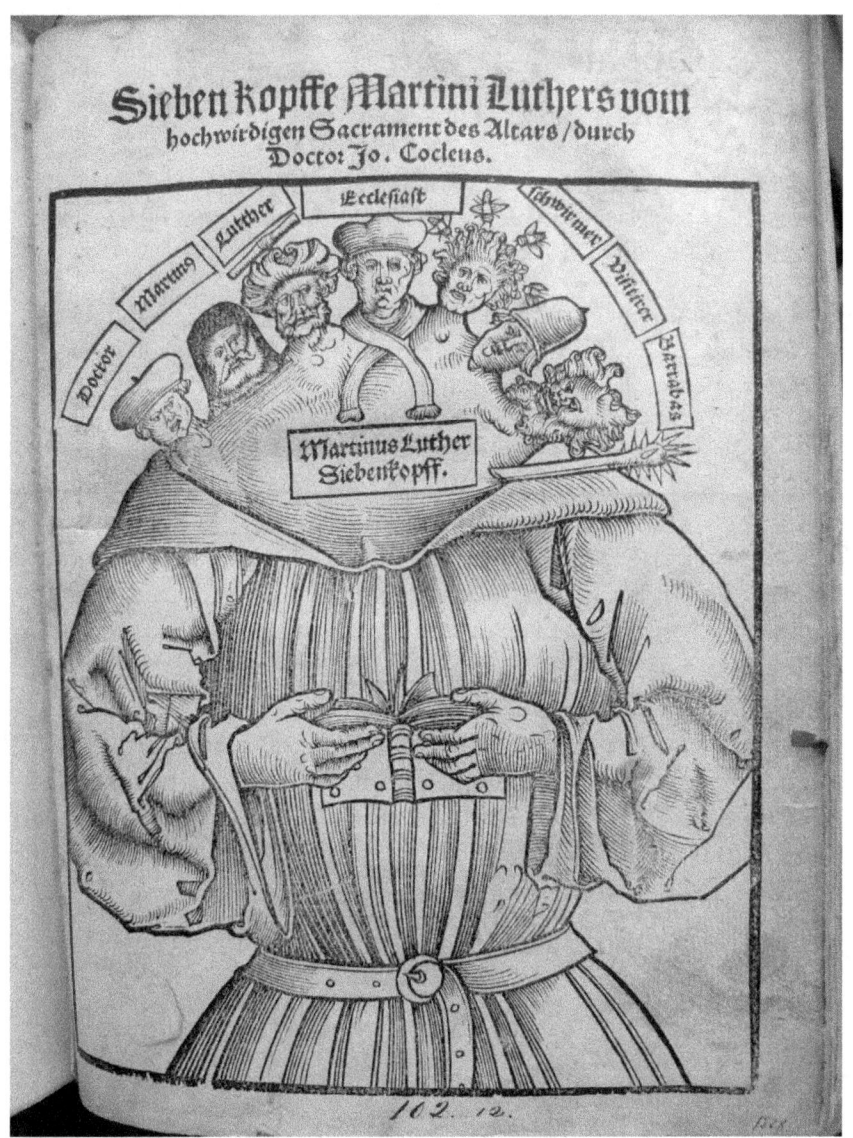

Doctor, Martinus, Lutther, Ecclesiast, Schwirmer, Visitirer, Barrabas
Luther as the seven-headed beast in the view of his adversaries:
learned, keen on church discipline, dangerous, confused, heretic, traitor.
Hans Brosamer for Johann Cochlaeus (1529): *Sieben kopffe Martini Luthers*
Tr.Luth. 102(12), [Tübingen: Ulrich Morhart d.Ä.: c.1532], VD16 C 4393

3. The Pamphlet War, or: Cochlaeus versus Luther

> Das sie aber auffrur vnd empörung gesucht haben, des bistu die erste vnd hochste vrsach, durch vilfeltige anreytzung vnter falschem schein des Euangeliums vnd Christlicher fryheit.

> But that they have sought rebellion and uprising, you are the first and highest cause of this, through manifold incitements under the false appearance of the Gospel and of Christian freedom.[1]

1. Alongside Hieronymus Emser's Counter-Reformation press in Dresden, it was above all Johann Cochlaeus (1479–1552), one of Luther's most persistent and learned adversaries, who knew how to attack the Reformer with both effect and sophistication. A humanist scholar, theologian, and formidable controversialist, Cochlaeus devoted much of his career to defending the authority of the Church, in particular against the challenges posed by the Reformation.[2] Through his numerous polemical writings, he sought to denounce what he saw as the doctrinal errors and social dangers inherent in Luther's teaching. Among the most influential works was his *Commentaria de actis et scriptis Martini Lutheri* (1549), one of the earliest 'sustained' Catholic narratives of the Reformation and a key source for subsequent polemicists.[3] In his response to *Wider die Rotten*, Cochlaeus displays both his rhetorical skill and steadfast conviction that Luther's ideas threatened the stability of Christian society. The practice of thwarting, indeed defaming, the writings of the Reformation's protagonists through separated, newly arranged, and richly annotated reprints of their texts was mastered by Cochlaeus like scarcely anyone else (though the Wittenbergers, Luther and Justus Jonas, were no less skilled in this art). It was therefore no coincidence that he "took up the question of the Wittenberg theologian's role in

---

[1] Cochlaeus, *Antwort*, 1525, C1r. [Transl. R. M.]
[2] Gerhard Markert (2008) offers a concise life portrait in *Menschen um Luther. Eine Geschichte der Reformation in Lebensbildern*, Ostfildern, 262–65.
[3] Cf. Kaufmann (2024), 208.

the contemporary uprisings with particular intensity."[4] Accordingly, between 1525 and 1526 he published what was, at the time, Luther's most vulnerable work, *Wider die Rotten*. On the one hand, he separated it from the text with which it was originally connected, Luther's *Ermahnung zum Frieden*; on the other, he flanked it with additional, supposedly problematic writings from the Reformer's pen, as well as with his own commentary to achieve for the public the ideological framing he intended.

Cochlaeus's primary focus was not by chance on *Wider die Rotten*, for this work promised to be easy prey, not only because of its brutally anti-peasant diction, but also because it lent itself to the public display of apparent contradictions in Luther's work. The aim was not argumentation, but rhetorical effect; not 'logic' and truth, but dominance of discourse – the core of a media strategy that relied not on mutual understanding, but on suppression and exclusion, resembling what today is referred to as 'cancel culture'.[5] In order to inform the common people more effectively (*zu besser vnterrichtung gemeynes volcks*) about the Peasants' War disaster, he published Luther's "small book" against the rebellious peasants (*Luthers buchlein, so er widder die auffrurigen Bawrn hat lassen auß geen* = *Wider die Rotten*), as he explains in his preface, so that "the common man might finally perceive and understand how Luther at first incited the good people with words to rebellion, to storm abbeys and monasteries",[6] yet later, when he realised "that they had turned badly violent, sided with the princes,

---

[4] Kaufmann (2024), 207, cf. generally 207–11. (All translations from secondary literature by R. M.)

[5] In the next edition of the *Reformation Pamphlets* in the *Treasures of the Taylorian*, which will focus on the anonymous *An die Versammlung der gemeinen Bauernschaft*, the problem of cancel culture in the Reformation will be addressed in greater detail. For the media campaign of the Counter-Reformation, cf. Kaufmann (2024), 200–14; for the Wittenbergers' publicist campaign against their critics, cf. Kaufmann (2024), 215–29.

[6] [Transl. R. M.] Cochlaeus, *Antwort*, 1525, AIV: *der gemeine man zu letzt merken und versteen soll, wye Luther das gut volck lang vorher mit worten zu auffrur, Stifft und klöster sturmen geraytzt habe.*

whom he had often defiled and made hated by the people", while "he now scolds and mistreats, most horribly, the poor, miserable, and wretchedly slain peasant folk, whom he had so fiercely incited and driven in many books (*in vil buchern*) for such a scheme."[7]

Like Emser, Cochlaeus saw the principal evil in Luther's argument for universal priesthood, through which, as Emser put it, laymen were made priests, priests laymen, princes peasants, and peasants in turn princes and free lords.[8] The uprising of the common man, Emser was convinced, had its origin in Luther's ideas. From the latter's proclamation of the freedom of a Christian followed not only the pernicious principle of the congregation, according to which a parish community might itself judge matters of doctrine and choose its own pastor,[9] and which the peasants and their leaders further radicalised into their principle of brotherhood, but, above all, rebellious attitudes among subjects against both clerical and feudal authorities. The most striking example of this was Müntzer's interpretation of Luther's idea of freedom. The Peasants' War confirmed for many of the Reformer's opponents, particularly in the Catholic camp, the destructive character of this new evangelical message. No doubt there were strong voices claiming that he was responsible not only for the catastrophe at Frankenhausen, but more broadly for the wave of peasant uprisings across the country. To Johann Cochlaeus, the uprising stood as direct evidence of the social and spiritual chaos unleashed by Luther's own 'revolt'.

---

[7] [Transl. R. M.] Cochlaeus, *Antwort*, 1525, Aɪv: *das sie vbel drobfaren, slecht er sich zun fursten, welche er vor vilmals grewlich geschendet vnd dem volck hessig gemacht hat, und schelt und schendet yetz vffs aller grewlichst das arm vnselig und iemerlich erslagen Bawrs volck, welchs er vor zu solcher spil in vil buchern hefftiglich gehetzet und getryben hat.*
[8] Cf. Kaufmann (2024), 206; A. Laube/H. W. Seiffert (ed.), *Flugschriften der Bauernkriegszeit*, Berlin 1975, 360, 21–22.
[9] *WA* ɪɪ, esp. 411, 13 – 412, 4.

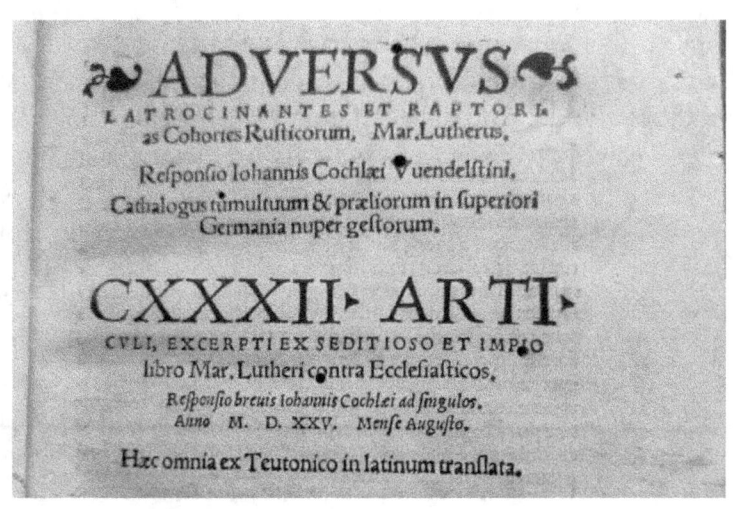

Titlepage of Cochlaeus' pamphlet, Douce C 302 (1)

2. At the end of July 1525, Johann Cochlaeus published *Wider die Reubischen und Mordischen Rotten der Bawren [...]. Antwort Johannis Coclei von Wendelstein*[10] in Cologne, his German response (*Antwort*) to Luther's tract *Wider die Rotten*, which had appeared almost three months earlier (early May 1525). The first edition contained, alongside Cochlaeus' reply to Luther, the chronological account *Eyn kurtzer begriff von auffruren vnd rotten der Bawrn in hohem Teutschland diß Jar begangen* ("A Brief Account of the Uprisings and Bands of Peasants in High Germany This Year"), a German translation of Johann Eck's *Fructus germinis Lutheris*,[11] intended to provide an overview of the peasant revolts across the country.[12] Although it was not explicitly noted that this was a translation or that the text originated

---

[10] Full title: *Wider die Reubischen und Mordischen rotten der Bawren die unter dem scheyn des heiligen Euangelions felschlichen wider alle Oberkeit sich setzen und empören Martinus Luther. Antwort Johannis Coclei von Wendelstein.*

[11] The text can be found in *Monumenta Germaniae Historica, Epistolae* I, Berlin 1891, 287. Cochlaeus altered Eck's sequence of reports several times in favour of a clearer overall structure according to region and chronology, Laube/Seiffert (1975), 613.

[12] Kaufmann (2024), 208, describes this as "something like the beginning of Peasants' War historiography".

with Eck, contemporary readers would likely have understood this, not least because Eck's authorship is made explicit in the concluding address to the *Fructus*. Also included, under the heading *Martinus Luther wider Thomas Muntzers Episteln*, was a brief extract, encompassing only a single printed page, from Luther's *Eine schreckliche Geschichte und Gericht Gottes über Thomas Müntzer* ("A Terrible History and God's Judgement on Thomas Müntzer")[13]. Cochlaeus concluded the volume with Luther's *Wider den falsch genannten geistlichen Stand des Papstes und der Bischöfe* ("Against the Falsely So-Called Spiritual Estate of the Pope and the Bishops")[14], from which he extracted 132 articles and provided answers to each from his perspective. The edition is dedicated to the mayors and councillors of Cologne.[15] Cochlaeus explains that he would have analysed Luther's misdeeds in even greater detail had he had Luther's books at hand, but he was, after all, only a guest in Cologne.[16] The pragmatic aim of the entire enterprise was to brand Luther's theses as seditious, anti-ecclesiastical, and highly dangerous to public order.

A Latin translation appeared one month later, on 30 August 1525. In addition to the Latin version of Cochlaeus' *Wider die Reubischen und Mordischen Rotten der Bawren*, now entitled *Adversus Latrocinantes et Raptorias Cohortes Rusticorum*, his treatment of Luther's *Wider den falsch genannten geistlichen Stand des Papstes und der Bischöfe* was likewise translated into Latin (*CXXXII Articuli, Excerpti ex Seditioso et Impio Libro Mar. Lutheri contra Ecclesiasticos*), and Eck's text was included as well, this time in the original Latin. The brief extract from Luther's text against Müntzer, however, was neither translated nor reprinted.

---

[13] *WA* 18, 362–74. Pamphlet held in the Taylorian: ARCH.80.G.1525(13).
[14] *WA* 10/II, 93–158.
[15] Cochlaeus, *Antwort*, 1525, Aiv.
[16] Cf. Laube/Seiffert (1975), 609.

The Pamphlet War xxxvii

Both of Cochlaeus' texts, the German first edition *Wider die Rotten* and the Latin version *Adversus Latrocinantes*, are furnished with marginal notes. The majority of the Latin marginalia are, to be sure, simple translations of the German glosses, differing only occasionally in minor details.[17] Yet there are also notable divergences. Some of the German marginalia were not translated into Latin or were replaced by glosses of different content. An example is the marginal note "Luther bluthdorstig" ("Luther bloodthirsty")[18], which in the Latin edition, at the corresponding place, reads *Luther contra [contru] merita sanctorum*[19], thereby highlighting a different aspect (*Luther opposing the merits of the saints*).

German marginal note *Luther bluthdorstig* in Cochlaeus, *Antwort*, 1525, C4v
(Bayerische Staatsbibliothek, 4 Polem. 632 t, Public domain)

Latin marginal note *Lutherus contra merita sanctorum* in
Cochlaeus *Adv. Latr.*, 1525, C2r, Douce C 302 (1)

---

[17] Thus, the German marginal note *wie scedlich Luter ißt* (B2v), for example, is rendered in Latin as *quam perniciosus populo Luther* (B1v). The addition of *populo* explicitly emphasises Luther's danger to the people, which appears to have been inserted for the sake of greater precision.
[18] Cochlaeus, *Antwort*, 1525, C4v.
[19] Cochlaeus, *Adversus Latrocinantes*, 1525, C2r.

This is by no means accidental, since the two languages were directed at different audiences and thus served different purposes. The vernacular was addressed to a broader public, and the commentary (drawing on the traditional language of the *artes*) primarily concerned with 'rhetoric' (*movere*). The learned language, by contrast, was aimed at an educated readership, and its commentary therefore more concerned with 'logic' (*docere*), thereby, at least in appearance, simulating a doctrinal disputation (*doctrina* vs. *persuasio*).[20] As for the Latin translation of the main text, it follows the German version quite faithfully, without abridgement or addition.

A year later, in June 1526, another edition of Cochlaeus's German response (*Antwort*) to Luther's *Wider die Rotten* appeared, this time without the texts that had accompanied it previously and instead including a reprint of Luther's *Sendbrief vom harten Büchlein wider die Bauern*, which Cochlaeus annotated with extended marginal notes and supplemented with both a preface and a concluding address.[21] In the preface, he refers to Luther's "three little books" (*drey buchlein*) about the peasants, by which he means the *Ermahnung zum Frieden* (April 1525), *Wider die Rotten* (May 1525), and the *Sendbrief vom harten Büchlein* (July 1525). He devotes the greater part of his preface to

---

[20] In the Latin version, a marginal note reads *contra principatus* (B1v), thereby highlighting Luther's opposition to the authorities; in the German edition, however, the note *Luters vntreu gegenn seinenn gleubigen* (B2v) appears instead, emphasising rather the emotional aspect associated with the term *Untreue* ("faithlessness", "betrayal").

[21] Laube and Seiffert's claim (1975, 609) that Cochlaeus' edition with the *Sendbrief vom harten Büchlein wider die Bauern* represents the original version is not correct. Since Luther's *Sendbrief vom harten Büchlein* did not go to press until the end of July 1525 (cf. WA 18, 377; by 1 August Spalatin had several copies of the edition), roughly contemporaneous with Cochlaeus' dedication to the German *Antwort*, it is chronologically unlikely that Cochlaeus could have referred to Luther's *Sendbrief vom harten Büchlein*. The fact that the Latin translation, which appeared only a month later, likewise responds solely to Luther's *Wider den falsch genannten geistlichen Stand des Papstes und der Bischöfe*, and not to the *harte Büchlein*, provides further evidence against this. Kaufmann (2024, 209) also dates Cochlaeus' edition containing his response to the *harte Büchlein* to June 1526, i.e., the following year, indicating that this edition must have been a subsequent issue rather than the original version.

quoting several passages from Luther's *Ermahnungsschrift*, in particular from its address to the princes (*An die Fürsten und Herrn*)[22], in order then, by reprinting once again his *Antwort* to Luther's *Wider die Rotten*, to expose Luther's 'change of course' as hypocrisy. The volume concludes with Luther's final publication on the subject, his *Sendbrief vom harten Büchlein*, in which, following the disasters at Böblingen (12 May), Frankenhausen (15 May), and Saverne (17 May),[23] he sought to justify the severity for which *Wider die Rotten* had been criticised. This text, with its demonstrative self-righteousness, fits perfectly with the disconnected publication of *Wider die Rotten*. By printing several excerpts from the *Ermahnung zum Frieden*, followed by his 'dialogically' staged response to *Wider die Rotten*, and finally Luther's *Sendbrief vom harten Büchlein*, annotated with his own commentary, Cochlaeus succeeds in framing Luther's three writings in line with his own objectives.

In his concluding address, Cochlaeus reiterates a number of points already made in his *Antwort*, above all Luther's subversion of authority, his deception of the people, and the suffering he thereby brought upon them. A striking passage reads:

> After the monk [i.e., Luther] has led the poor people into such a pitiful undertaking, he gives them the devil's reward. […] He has stirred the common man to disobedience and rebellion with a false freedom of baptism and the Gospel; now he writes, "hew, stab, strike, as long as a vein still stirs!"[24] He has written so much confused disputation about faith that he has made almost all the people of the German nation erring and doubtful in their belief. […] Now there is nothing left in heaven or on earth that this giant (*Gygant*) does not attack, except for the throne of divine majesty itself. On earth, the Holy Roman Church is for him a red Babylonian whore; the pope, an Antichrist; the emperor, a sack of worms; the princes,

---

[22] *WA* 18, 293–99.
[23] The most infamous bloodbaths carried out under princely authority.
[24] It is a montage of either *WA* 18, 358, 14–15, or ibid., 361, 25 (or both), with *WA* 18, 314, 15–16.

foolish tyrants and simpletons; the bishops, idols and carnival puppets; the priests, monks, and nuns, temple servants, hypocrites, and intolerable burdens upon the earth, etc.[25]

The argumentative focus quite deliberately falls on Luther's highly controversial notion of freedom. Cochlaeus is keen to emphasise its 'negative' aspect, namely, the loosening of all worldly bonds, without acknowledging the 'positive' side that Luther, in his reading of the Gospel (indeed, of the whole New Testament), considers equally important. Of course, mentioning the positive aspect of 'Lutheran' freedom might seem unnecessary, since in *Wider die Rotten* Luther himself does not address any longer what this entails within the Kingdom of God (love, service, and suffering), but focuses exclusively on the consequences of disobedience within the Kingdom of the World (punishment, repression, and judgment).[26] It was, however, no coincidence that Cochlaeus ignored the broader literary context of the *Ermahnungsschrift*, addressing it only selectively. Luther's concept, entirely unproblematic in terms of political order, which defined the positive aspect of freedom not as a spiritual mandate for encroachment (*fides efficax*), but precisely as a humble restraint against it (*fides imputativa*), since the former would, in his view, amount to nothing but self-righteousness (Müntzer), as the Kingdom of God is realised *in* the world as suffering *from* the world, is deliberately suppressed by Cochlaeus. Naturally, highlighting the positive side of Lutheran

---

[25] [Transl. R. M.] Cochlaeus, *Antwort*, 1526, F4v–G1r: *Nach dem der Munch das arm volck in solchs yemerlich spil gefuret hat / gibt er im des Teufels lon / [...] / hat den gemeynen man mit falscher freiheit der tauff und Euangeliums zu vngehorsam vnd auffrur erreget / yetz schreibt er / haw / stich / schlahe / als lang sich eyn ader reget / Hat so vil verwyrrets disputiren von glauben geschryben / biß daz er schier alles volck Teutscher Nation irr vnd tzweyflich im glauben gemacht hat. [...] Nu ist nichts mer vorhanden / im hymel vnd auff erden das disser Gygant nit bestreitet / außgenomen denn Thron gottlicher Maiestat / auff erden ist yme die heylig Romisch kirch ein rote Byblonische hur / der babst eyn antichrist / der keyser ein madensack / die fursten narren tyranen vnd maulaffen / die bischof ölgotzen vnd fastnacht putzen / die priester munch vnd nonnen Tempelknecht, gleyßner / vntrechliche purde der erden etc.*
[26] Cf. *WA* 18, 389, 14–24.

freedom would have undermined his argument, and would have required him to engage in the debate with an attitude of mutual understanding. Cochlaeus goes so far as to accuse Luther of having, like Arius (*mit Arrio*), denied the divinity of Christ by claiming that Luther's soul detested the word *Homousion* (ὁμοούσιον τῷ πατρί, *consubstantialem Patri*)[27], which signifies the consubstantiality of Christ, the Son, with God the Father[28] – an entirely specious claim.

The Latin translation of the work is dedicated to the Bishop of Rochester, John Fisher (1469–1535). Fisher, Chancellor of the University of Cambridge and formerly tutor to the young Henry VIII, under whom he would later be charged with high treason and executed just days before Thomas More, was among the first opponents of Luther in England.[29] Most notable among his works is the extensive *Assertionis Lutheranae Confutatio* (1523), written in response to Luther's *Assertio Omnium Articulorum* (1520). In the *Confutatio*, Fisher stages a quasi-fictional dialogue between himself and the German reformer, working systematically through Luther's text and responding to its arguments piece by piece. Cochlaeus, a great admirer of Fisher (and ridiculed for his English connections by Luther and Jonas)[30], whom he described as "the greatest Catholic theologian in England at the time", who "most seriously and thoroughly refuted the two principal leaders among the heretics of this time, Luther and Oecolampadius", structures his own response (*Antwort*) to Luther's *Wider die Rotten* in

---

[27] Cochlaeus, *Antwort*, 1526, F4v: *mit Arrio geschmehet so er spricht / Mein sele hasset daz wort Homousion welchs bedeut / daz Christus sey eyns gottlichen wesens mit gott dem vatter*.
[28] Cf. Council of Constantinople, 381 (*Constantinopolitanum*).
[29] According to Germain Marc'hadour, he was also "the first theologian to diagnose justification through faith alone as the founding dogma of the Protestant Reformation". Cf. Germain Marc'hadour (2010), 'Review of Erasmus' Defence of his De libero arbitrio', *Moreana* 47 (181–82), 293–302, here 299.
[30] Cf. *Epistola D. Coclei ad Georgium Wicelium* (Wittenberg, 1534), B1v–B2v: "a man so concerned for both the churches of England and their gold" (*homini, de Ecclesiis Angliae simul et de auro valde solicito*).

a similar way, following Fisher's model.[31] In his dedication, Cochlaeus explicitly refers to Fisher's *Confutatio*, praising his efforts against Luther while lamenting that his work was not accessible to Germans in their own language. He translated two of its articles into German, but, he notes, a reliable printer was lacking to publish the work in full. He also recounts that he had recently suffered an act of sabotage by Lutherans: his attempt to print the two articles he had translated, together with a treatise by Johann Dietenberg, failed because the Lutherans, taking advantage of the Strasbourg censorship system, had secretly swapped his printed sheets, thereby falsifying both works.[32] Not by chance, all of this recalls a practice in the strategic spirit of a cancel culture deliberately disengaged from (understanding-oriented)[33] communication.

3. Cochlaeus's *Antwort*, arranged in a thesis–antithesis structure, follows Luther's statements, which Cochlaeus numbers from I to XXXI, responding more or less extensively to each. It becomes clear that the author of these 'answers' was an outstanding connoisseur of Luther's work: in this work alone, by 1525, he was able to draw upon more than twenty of the Reformer's writings and sermons to expose his opponent's 'hypocrisy'. Cochlaeus had already employed the 'dialogical' form in earlier works against Luther, for instance in his 1525 Strasbourg-printed *Antwort Johan Cochleus auff .xci. artickelen / uß dreien Sermonen M. Luth. gezogen*. In this, as in those others, John Fisher's *Confutatio*, which addressed Luther's *Assertio Omnium Articulorum*, very likely served as a model. Cochlaeus's *Antwort* sought to demonstrate that Luther should be regarded as the spiritual instigator of the Peasants' War, and that his peasant-critical remarks in *Wider die Rotten* were therefore two-faced and opportunistic. His *Antwort* is shaped above all by the following arguments, to which he

---

[31] Cf. Thomas P. Scheck (2013), "John Fisher's Response to Martin Luther", in: *Franciscan Studies*, Vol. 71, 463–509, here: 463–64.
[32] Cf. Cochlaeus, *Adversus Latrocinantes*, 1525, A1v–A2r.
[33] Cf. Jürgen Habermas (²1997), *Theorie des kommunikativen Handelns*, Vol. 1, Frankfurt a. M., 412–50, esp. 412–14.

repeatedly returns: (*i.*) Luther had seduced the poor, simple people through his "false freedom" (*falsche freiheit*) and was thus the cause of all uprisings and the suffering that accompanied them. (*ii.*) He is a hypocrite and a liar, who first railed against the authorities and attacked them with the utmost vehemence, only to later switch sides and speak with bloodthirsty (*bluthdorstig*) cruelty against the peasants. (*iii.*) Through his earlier criticism of princes and authorities, the peasants had lost all respect for both Church and secular rulers, came to despise them, and eventually rebelled. Moreover, Luther was unwilling to take up arms in defense of his own cause. He was even worse than Müntzer, argues Cochlaeus, since the latter had never had anywhere near the same influence as Luther and had wreaked havoc only in Thuringia, whereas Luther had set the entire country aflame.

> Furthermore, you have caused and provoked a thousand times more harm, temptation, and outrage than Müntzer. Why? Well, Müntzer only carried out his mischief in Thuringia, whereas you have stirred up unrest throughout the entire German nation.[34]

Some examples from his *Antwort* illustrate his rhetorical approach in opposing Luther. Without justifying their uprisings, Cochlaeus rejects Luther's condemnation of the peasants for their use of violence and refers to *Ad Dialogum Silvestri Prieratis* (1518)[35] and *An den christlichen Adel deutscher Nation* (1520)[36] to show that Luther himself had, in the past (*vor vier oder funf iaren*), "desired the fist" (*der faust begert*), as the marginal note to the passage aptly summarises, to take up arms against the pope, cardinals, and all the clergy, and to wash one's hands in their blood (*mit allerley waffen Babst, Cardinael vnd alle geistlikeit*

---

[34] [Transl. R. M.] Cochlaeus, *Antwort*, 1525, C2r: *dann du Tausent mal mer schadens vnd verfurens vnd empörung im volck getan vnd erregt haßt, dann der Muntzer. wie so? also. Muntzer hat alleyn in Turingen rumort. du haßt alle landt Teutscher Nation vol rumors gemacht.*
[35] *WA* 1, 644–86.
[36] *WA* 6, 381–469.

anfallen, vnd die hende in yrem blut waschen).[37] Elsewhere, he reproaches him for having insulted the authorities before the people and for having publicly spread his contempt for the princes. Luther is quoted in no. VIII as saying: "Which is also why Saint Paul passes this judgement on them, saying in Romans 13 [2]: 'Those who resist authority will bring judgement upon themselves.' These words will eventually, sooner or later, hit their mark with the peasants as well, because God wants loyalty (*trew*) and duty (*pflicht*) to be observed."[38] Cochlaeus' response (*Antwort*) to this reads as follows:

> But then, you should not have prescribed the very opposite (*widerspil*) to the poor, simple people! You should have kept your wretched freedom (*lausige fryheit*) tucked away in your cowl at home! You should not have set the lice upon the people's skin when you write how strictly one is bound to be obedient to the authorities! You should not have called the emperor a sack of worms, and the princes lewd fools, simpletons, senseless and raging madmen, and tyrants! You should not have declared the Turk ten times wiser and more pious than our princes! You should not have written publicly that God would deliver us from them [i.e., the princes] and grant us other rulers! You should not so often have threatened them with that word of the psalmist: *He has poured out contempt upon princes!*[39] You should not have spread such, and many other similar, sayings and wicked incitements against the authorities[40] among the people! Then we would have been spared this misery and bloodshed.[41]

---

[37] Cochlaeus, *Antwort*, 1525, A2v (VD16 L 7485).
[38] Cf. *WA* 18, 357, 29–358, 2.
[39] Ps 107:40. "He poureth contempt upon princes, and causeth them to wander in the wilderness, where there is no way". (KJV)
[40] Cf. *WA* 11 (*Von weltlicher Obrigkeit*), 267–70.
[41] [Transl. R. M.] Cochlaeus, *Antwort*, 1525, B1r–v (VD16 L 7485): *Du soltest aber darvor nicht das widerspil dem armen einfeltigenn volck furgeschryben habenn. Soltest dein lausige fryheit in deiner kutten da heymbd behalten haben. Soltest nit die leuß dem volck an den peltz gesetzt haben, do du schrybst, wie serr man schuldigh sey der Oberkeit gehorsam zu seyn. Soltest nit dem keyser eyn Madensack, vnd die fursten vnzuchtlich Narren, Maulaffen, vnsynnige vnd rasende wueterer vnd Tyrannen geheissen haben. Soltest nit den*

The passage employs repeated exclamatory "You should not have" statements, building to a quasi-conditional conclusion, not only to morally censure the author, Luther, but also to render his position absurd, while at the same time defending established authority. It is not by chance that Cochlaeus' *Antwort*, to begin with, evokes Luther's concept of freedom, for that is precisely his aim: to present it as the very root of evil, from which all other evils then proceed, some of which he specifies. The motif of "false freedom" forms the pivot at the level of argumentation and thus functions as the all but undisguised central theme of Cochlaeus' critique. In no. II, commenting on Luther's opening remark about the peasants: "But before I even have time to look round, off they go, taking matters violently into their own hands, forgetting their offer, thieving, and running riot like mad dogs",[42] Cochlaeus, as part of a longer statement, answers: "You have so long and so vehemently preached and prescribed to the poor people, falsely, the Word of God and Christian freedom, that you have driven them utterly mad and out of their senses."[43]

In the course of his remarks on no. III of his *Antwort*, which includes the quote, "From this we can now clearly see the deception they intended and that what they proposed in the *Twelve Articles* in the name

---

Turken zehen mal kluger vnd frummer, dan vnsere fursten seind, geachtet haben. Soltest nit offentlig geschryben haben Got wolle vns von ynen erledigen vnd andre regenten geben. Soltest nit so oft wyder sie gedrewt haben auff diß wort der psalmisten: Er hat auß geschutt verachtung vber die fursten. Solche vnd der gleichen vil andre spruche vnd böße anreytzung wider die Oberkeit, soltestu nit in das volck haben außgeprait. So weren wyr yetz solchs iamers vnd blutvergiessens vertragen.

[42] Cf. *WA* 18, 357, 6–9.
[43] [Transl. R. M.] Cochlaeus, *Antwort*, 1525, A3r: *Ir habt dem armen volck so lang vnd so hefftig furgepredigt vnd vur furgeschryben felschlich von gots wort vnnd Christlicher fryheit, bys das yr gar tobend vnnd vnsynnich gemacht hab.* Concluding the paragraph, again focusing on the problematic concept of freedom, it reads: "[...] while you daub false freedom before it [i.e., the people] as something delightfully sweet" (*die weyl ir ime die falschen freyheit so suß ein streichet*).

of the Gospel was nothing but lies",[44] Cochlaeus refers to Luther's *De captivitate Babylonica ecclesiae*:

> For then, four years ago, you wrote in the *Babylonian Captivity*: 'I also faithfully proclaim', you say, "that no Christian may be bound by any kind of law, neither by men nor by angels, except to the extent they wish, as we are free from all of them (i.e., those laws)." Likewise, you have since advanced the same argument in many other books and sermons addressed to the people.[45]

Cochlaeus seems to suggest that this is a direct quotation, which it is not, since it is, at best, a montage of two distinct passages. No corresponding statement can be found anywhere in Luther's treatise. What can be found, however, are the phrases *verbis divinis non est ulla facienda vis, neque per hominem neque per angelum* ("no force of any kind must be applied to the divine words, neither by a human nor by an angel")[46] and *nullum eis esse super nos ius imperii, nisi quantum nos sponte nostra admitteremus* ("that they have no right of authority over us, except insofar as we of our own accord grant it to them")[47]. The corresponding Latin passage reads:

> *Clamo (inquis) fideliter quoque, nullo iure posse Christianis vllam imponi legem neque ab hominibus neque ab Angelis, nisi quantum voluerint. Quia liberi sumus ab ijs omnibus. Similiter in plerisque alijs libris sermonibusque populo multa in hanc sententiam proposuisti.*
>
> "I also faithfully proclaim", you say, "that by no right can any law be imposed on Christians, neither by men nor by angels, except to the extent they wish, since we are free from all of them". Similarly, in most of the other books and sermons, you have proposed many

---

[44] Cf. *WA* 18, 357, 9–12.
[45] [Transl. R. M.] Cochlaeus, *Antwort*, 1525, A3r–v: *dan also hastu vor vier Jarn geschryben in der Babylonischen gefencknuß. Ich ruff auch getrewlich, sprichstu, das mit keynen rechten den Christen mag vffgelegt werden eincherlei gesatz, weder von menschen, noch von Engeln, dan so vil sy wöllen, wan wir seind frey von inenn allen. Der gleichen hastu auch her nach in vil andern Buchern vnd predigen dem volck furgeben.*
[46] *WA* 6, 509, 8–9.
[47] *WA* 6, 564, 8–9.

things to the people in line with this view.⁴⁸

The Latin edition of his *Antwort* from the end of August is faithfully translated and offers nothing new; the marginal notes, too, are accurately reproduced; here, first, that Luther speaks with two tongues (*Luter hat zwu zungen – Bilinguis Lutherus*), and second, that one is dealing here with Luther's false freedom (*falsche fryheit des Luthers – Falsa libertas Lutheri*).

Cochlaeus quotes and translates the paragraphs he has numbered with relative accuracy, whereas in the antithetically arranged commentaries he tends to paraphrase, omitting and distorting aspects; perhaps, as he himself notes, because he did not have the necessary books at hand and thus had to work from memory (he was, according to his own account, in Cologne); but perhaps also deliberately, in order to construct the desired 'narrative'. That his references to Luther's work were selective should come as no surprise and is already evident in his exclusion of the *Ermahnungsschrift*, which provides the crucial context for *Wider die Rotten*.

In another passage, in no. XI,⁴⁹ he confronts Luther with the harm he has brought upon the land and calls his victory over the deluded peasants the Devil's, an 'argument' that Luther himself had employed against the papal Church, the peasants, and their leaders, especially Müntzer. In addition, he turns Luther's accusation that the rebellious peasants left behind widows and orphans back on him: applying it to Luther himself.

> Now you have prevailed (*gewunnen*): you have handed over to the Devil more than a hundred thousand peasants (oh, what misery, what wretchedness!), body and soul; you have made countless people widows and orphans; you have robbed the poor folk, through a number of useless and harmful books, of more money than all the indulgence-mongers, as you call them, managed to do

---

⁴⁸ Cochlaeus, *Adversus Latrocinantes*, 1525, A3r.
⁴⁹ Addressing *WA* 18, 358, 8–14.

in twenty or thirty years; and you have brought this rebellion upon the land, through which princes and their subjects alike have been led into immeasurable harm.[50]

One finds, here as elsewhere, the typical rhetorical structure of staccato parallelism, which allows for no further argument and appeals to emotion, thereby relying on the sheer givenness of what is supposed to be 'the truth'. In terms of content, Cochlaeus continually revisits the same points, bringing the same aspects into focus. Plato (in his *Gorgias*) would have called this style sophistic, though it should not be forgotten that Luther himself knew very well how to operate as a sharp-tongued sophist.[51]

Cochlaeus comments on perhaps the best-known passage from *Wider die Rotten*: "And so, dear lords, come and redeem, come and rescue, come and help, have mercy on these poor folk! Whoever can do so, come and stab, strike, and strangle! If you die in doing so, good for you: a more blessed death you can never achieve, for you die in obedience to God's word and command [...]."[52] as follows (no. XIX):

Ah, how merciful[53] you are, and at once so cruel to the peasants

---

[50] [Transl. R. M.] Cochlaeus, *Antwort*, 1525, B2v: *Nu hastu gewunnen, hast dem Teufel mer dan hundert Tausent Bawrn (o des iamers vnd elends) mit leib vnd seel vbergeben, hast witwen vnd weysen on zal gemagt, hast das arm volck zu vor mit vil vnnutzen vnnd schedlichen buchern vmb mer geltz bracht, dan alle Ablaßkremer, wie du sie nennest, in xx. oder xxx. iarn gethan haben, hast disse auffrur ins landt gebracht, dar durch die fursten mitsampt yren unterthanen in vnermeßlichen schaden gefurt seind.*

[51] The sophist is concerned not with truth, but with persuasion alone. In the tradition of the *artes liberales*, however, rhetoric was still understood as the art of persuading in the service of truth secured by logic – a truth that, through the use of stylistic means, was then intended to be communicated beyond expert circles. Rhetoric, in other words, was the 'pragmatic' instrument of logic. Cf. Rahel Micklich, *Spekulative Pädagogik. Johannes de Garlandia auf den Spuren des Alanus ab Insulis*, Brussels 2025, 75–97.

[52] Cf. *WA* 18, 361, 24–27, translation taken from our edition below, A4r.

[53] Luther had argued that it was also an act of mercy to remove those who, lawlessly and without mercy, strike out, in order to protect those who suffer such injustice, that is, to show mercy to them. Although this is not yet the argument of *Wider die*

[…]! But if it is indeed such a good and beatifying work to put the poor, misled peasants to death by stabbing, smiting, and slaying them, why did you not yourself join in and strike into their ranks? If you are permitted to take a wife, then surely you might also have been permitted to take a pike or a sword in your hand, even though you are a monk. Yes, if all this could be accomplished by writing and empty words alone, you would be the very best of all and would devour the peasants at a single stroke.[54]

Somewhat surprisingly, the commentary on this passage is relatively brief, even though it seems the perfect prey for sharper attack. Measured against Luther, he falls short of the latter's force. Above all, the accusation against the Reformer, that he was unwilling to dirty his own hands and sought to wage his battle solely within public discourse, is not very convincing. What stands out, as elsewhere, is once again the cynical tone.

This profile of Cochlaeus's pamphlet war against Luther, exemplified by his German and Latin response to *Wider die Rotten*, should suffice to convey an impression of how Luther's fierce tract, controversial even within his own ranks, was received by the Catholic Counter-Reformation, led by figures such as Emser and Cochlaeus. It should now be clear that the peasants, stylised as 'victims', were never truly meant as such, but were instrumentalised to serve ecclesiastico-political interests, namely to bring the Reformation down, or at least to weaken it. The suffering of the peasants was, indeed, exploited in a

---

Rotten (May 1525), it becomes central to his *Sendbrief vom harten Büchlein wider die Bauern* (July 1525), in which he responds, among other things, alongside the accusation of having fallen into works-righteousness, to the charge of having been unmerciful. Cf. *WA* 18, 390, 20–35.

[54] [Transl. R. M.] Cochlaeus, *Antwort*, 1525, Dıv: *Ey wie barmhertzich vnd bo͞ßbewrisch bistu itz […]. So es aber so eyn gut selig werckt ist, die arme verfurten bawrn zu todt stechen, slahen vnd wurgen, warumb bistu nicht auch myt gezogen vnd hast yn hauffen geslagen, darfstu ein weyb nemen, du dorffest auch wol eyn speiß ader ein swerdt in die faust nemen, wie wol du ein Munch bist, ya wens alles mit schreiben vnd vnnutzen worten were auß gericht, so werstu wol der aller beste, vnd wurdest die bawnr all fressen auff eyn mael.*

ruthless battle shaped by a climate of cancel culture, in which truth and justice were by no means the foremost concern, but rather the quasi-communicative spoils of the culture war raging in those years between Wittenberg and Rome.

Cochlaeus in Oxford: *Adversus Latrocinantes* and its 'Companions'[55]

The Bodleian Library holds three copies of Cochlaeus's Latin response to Luther, each of which includes the two other works from the Cologne edition with which it was commonly printed: Johannes Eck's *Fructus germinis Lutheri* and Cochlaeus's Latin translation and commentary on Luther's *Wider den geistlichen Stand*.

Under the shelfmark Douce C 302 (1) can be found a copy of the complete Cologne edition, bound together with another of Cochlaeus's works, his *Articuli CCCCC Martini Lutheri* (Cologne, 1526), in which Cochlaeus replies to five hundred articles extracted from Luther's sermons, employing his familiar 'dialogical' method. The quarto volume, bound in a late eighteenth- or early nineteenth-century binding and titled *Cochlaeus Contra Lutherum. 1525–1526*, comes from the library of Francis Douce (1757–1834), a merchant and lawyer best known as an avid book collector, who bequeathed his entire collection of manuscripts, printed books, coins, and prints to the Bodleian Library.[56] Apart from one lengthy marginal note in sermon XXXV, article 491, and a few pencil markings in Cochlaeus's *Articuli CCCCC Martini Lutheri*, no other contemporary annotations are present.

The other Bodleian volume, also in quarto, is listed under the shelfmark Tr. Luth. 44 (103). The volume is bound in an early nineteenth-century Bodleian binding under the title *Autographa Reformatorum*.

---

[55] Many thanks to Colin Harris, former Superintendent of the Bodleian's Special Collections Reading Rooms, for his generous and insightful comments on the Bodleian's book-historical holdings.
[56] Cf. https://digital.bodleian.ox.ac.uk/collections/douce/.

Anni 1525. Numero 94–106. Tratt. Luth. XLIV. The provenance of the volume is unknown. It was rebound by the Bodleian, but the original order of the texts was retained. The carefully curated selection of writings it contains must once have belonged to a single owner. The volume comprises thirteen Reformation pamphlets and writings, authored by both Protestants and Catholics (seven Catholic, six Protestant), covering a wide range of subjects—from the Peasants' War to infant baptism and the Schwärmer (enthusiasts, spiritualists)—as well as several works condemning or arguing against Luther's writings and statements, and by Protestants concerning Papist misdeeds. All the works included in the volume were printed in 1525; for most, this was the year of their first publication, whereas John Fisher's *Assertio*, of course, had first appeared in 1523. Consequently, the Peasants' War is among the most prominent subjects represented.

The collection includes a pamphlet by (1) Sebastian Lotzer (*Entschuldigung ainer frummen Christlichen Gemain zu Memmingen / Apology of a Pious Christian Community in Memmingen*); a dialogue by (2) Johannes Lang, although he is not named as the author in the pamphlet, concerning the so-called *Schwärmer* (*Ain nützlicher Dialogus [...] zwischen ainen münzerischen Schwermer vnd ainen euangelischen frummen Bauern / A Useful Dialogue [...] between a Münzerite Enthusiast and a Pious Evangelical Peasant*); a dialogue between a papist and an evangelical man by (3) Wenzeslaus Linck (*Dyalogus Der Außgelauffen Münch / Dialogue of the Runaway Monk*); an attempt at mediation between peasants and the authorities by (4) Hieronymus von Endorf (*Ain [...] prophetisch Schaydung, gantz unpartheysch, zwischen allenthalben auffrüriger Bawrschafft und jrer Herren / A [...] Prophetic Separation, Entirely Impartial, between the Rebellious Peasantry Everywhere and Their Lords*); (5) Johann Fundling's polemic against Luther (*Anzaigung zwayer falschen zungen des Luthers / Indication of Two False Tongues of Luther*); (6) Sigmund zu Hohenlohe's, the Domdechant of Strasbourg, admonition for clerical reform (*Creütz Biechlinn / Little Book of the Cross*); (7) a Wittenberg-printed translation of Pope Clement VII's *Bulla indictionis anni Jubilei proximi* (*Des*

Papstes Clemens des Siebenten zwei Bullen / *Two Bulls of Pope Clement VII*); (8) John Fisher's famous *Assertionis Lutheranae Confutatio*, which occupies half of the entire volume with its over six hundred pages; (9) Cochlaeus's *Articuli CCCCC Martini Lutheri*, followed by his (10) *Adversus Latrocinantes*; two works by Bartholomäus Arnoldi von Usingen, (11) *De Merito bonorum operum* / *On the Merit of Good Works* and (12) *De falsis prophetis* / *On False Prophets*, both directed against Protestant doctrine; and finally, a treatise by (13) Eberhard Weidensee on infant baptism (*Von dem stand der kindlein so on die tauff vorscheyden* / *On the State of Children Who Die Without Baptism*).

The third Bodleian volume containing Cochlaeus's response to Luther is held under the shelfmark C 2.10(3) Linc., in an intriguing early sixteenth-century binding. The binding, attributed to the Netherlands but later brought to England, depicts a flagellation scene. Only three examples of this type of binding are known to exist in England, making it particularly noteworthy. Basil Oldham, however, observed that "it is curious that the designer, who was able to convey so much movement in the flagellation scene, failed completely to draw the pavement in perspective."[57]

The volume contains six works: (1) Josse van Clichtove, or, in Latinised form, Jodocus Clichtoveus, *De veneratione sanctorum* (Paris, 1523); followed by two works by Johann Cochlaeus: (2) *Articuli CCCCC Martini Lutheri* (Cologne, 1525), which was often, as in this case, bound together with the previously discussed (3) *Adversus Latrocinantes*. Next comes the work of the Dominican and professor of theology Eustachius van der Rivieren, who styled himself Eustachius van Zichem: (4) *Sacramentorum brevis elucidatio* (Antwerp, 1523), a treatise directed against Luther and his more radical followers. The volume continues with two works printed by the renowned Parisian printer Jodocus Badius Ascensius: (5) *Determinatio Theologicae facul-*

---

[57] Cf. J. Basil Oldham (1958), *Blind Panels of English Binders*, Cambridge, 22.

tatis Parisiensis super Doctrina Lutheriana, in which 153 articles of Luther's teaching were condemned by the University of Paris; and finally, (6) Guillaume Budé's *De contemptu rerum fortuitarum libri tres*.

What is particularly noteworthy about this volume is that it once belonged to the "vociferously Protestant"[58] Thomas Barlow (1607–1691), Bishop of Lincoln, who bequeathed more than 6,000 volumes to the Bodleian Library.[59] With the exception of the final work, all writings in the volume are directed against Luther and his doctrine, and all six are of Catholic origin. A later hand, perhaps even that of Barlow himself, who was known occasionally to record the names of authors of anonymous tracts, has added the year of publication for those works lacking a printed date. Barlow's ownership of these fervently Catholic polemics is a curious irony: a staunchly anti-Catholic Anglican bishop, famous for denouncing the Pope as the Antichrist, preserving Catholic polemics.

The three *Sammelbände* with Cochlaeus' pamphlet
Bodleian Library, Tr. Luth. 44 / C 2.10 Linc. / Douce C 302

---

[58] Cf. https://archives.bodleian.ox.ac.uk/repositories/2/resources/7997.
[59] Cf. Karen Attar (ed.) (³2016), Directory of Rare Book and Special Collections in the UK and Republic of Ireland. Facet, 315.

Ausweichen vor der Reaktion. Das Verbrechen von Frankenhausen hat sich im Bewußtsein des Volkes bewahrt.

Luther, der sich in seinem häßlichen Pamphlet „Wider die mörderischen und räuberischen Rotten der Bauern" auf die Seite der Fürsten stellte, erblickte in der Niederlage der Aufrührer den Triumph Gottes über den Satan und eine Bestätigung dafür, daß Müntzer das Volk verführt hatte. Er rief dazu auf, zu würgen und zu stechen und sich mit Grausamkeit das Himmelreich zu verdienen. Das war der Tiefpunkt eines Weges, der 1517 so verheißungsvoll begonnen hatte.

Die Folter
Holzschnitt (Ausschnitt) von Hans Burgmair d. Ä.

Hans Burgkmair's woodcut of the torturing of peasants on the page for Luther's *Wider die Rotten*, Bensing (1965), 87, published by VEB Bibliographisches Institut.

2. The Pamphlet in the GDR
Timothy Powell

It should come as no surprise that *Wider die Rotten der Bauern*, one of Martin Luther's most rabid anti-peasant writings, was a particularly uncomfortable text for the historians and literary scholars of the German Democratic Republic – the self-styled "workers' and peasants state". GDR interpreters were horrified by Luther's calls for the rebellious peasants of 1525 to be stabbed, strangled and overcome by any means necessary by the nobility, and condemned the pamphlet as a hateful and angry tirade that went beyond the pale in every respect and definitively marked Luther's abandonment of the revolutionary cause.

Luther was a highly ambivalent figure in the GDR. Less favourable interpretations of Luther as a traitor to the peasants who prevented the Reformation from developing into a revolution prevailed in the 1950s.[1] However, the Wernigerode Conference of GDR early modern historians in 1960 shifted the focus of GDR Luther scholarship towards his 'progressive' period between the *95 Theses* in 1517 and the Diet of Worms in 1521.[2] This would shape official images of Luther around the Reformation anniversary in 1967, which strongly focused on these early 'progressive' years and explained the more uncomfortable aspects of his biography as products of his time and society.[3] Overall, Luther appears to have moved into the background of GDR historiography in the run-up to the Peasants' War anniversary in 1975. However, ahead of the quincentenary of his birth in 1983, he would be assigned a crucial role in GDR historical and cultural narratives as an individual who made an immense contribution to advancing what Marxist-Leninist ideology regarded as the historical and social progression that would reach its fulfilment in the 'socialist'

---

[1] Müller, Laurenz, *Diktatur und Revolution: Reformation und Bauernkrieg in der Geschichtsschreibung des 'Dritten Reiches' und der DDR* (Stuttgart: Lucius und Lucius, 2004), pp. 189, 202.
[2] Müller, pp. 212–14.
[3] Müller, pp. 225; 233–34.

society of the GDR.[4] Nevertheless, around the official commemorations of Martin Luther and the Reformation in 1967 and 1983, some attempts were made to partially rehabilitate it (and Luther as its author figure), seeking to make sense of its graphic calls for violence that had confounded earlier interpreters by attempting to situate the pamphlet within a variety of contexts that would at least enable it to be presented as a logical – although still extreme and unjustifiable – product of Luther's life, work and times.

GDR interpreters' perceptions of Luther's pamphlet (and the Peasants' War as a whole) were broadly shaped by two key Marxist historical writings, the first of which was *Der deutsche Bauernkrieg* (1850) by Friedrich Engels (1820–95), co-author with Karl Marx (1818–83) of *Das kommunistische Manifest* (1848).[5] Writing in the aftermath of the revolutions of 1848–49, Engels sees the strength of the German people beginning to flag after two years of struggle. He seeks to encourage them to continue by declaring that "[a]uch das deutsche Volk hat seine revolutionäre Tradition", urging them to draw fresh inspiration from the Peasants' War as a period of great revolutionary individuals and a people full of ideas and projects developing the strength and endurance to realise them. He establishes an historical parallel between the events of 1525 and those of 1848–49, arguing that the two conflicts are not as distant from each other as they may seem – especially as far as "the enemies to be fought" by the people are concerned.

Engels argues that rapid but highly localised economic development had led to equally rapid change in the society of the German-speaking lands, accelerating the decline of the ruling classes and the rise of new social groups, and splintering it into numerous aristocratic, bourgeois, clerical and 'plebeian' sub-groups, with almost the entire edifice resting on the backs of the peasants. However, he states that

---

[4] Müller, pp. 260–61.
[5] Friedrich Engels (1960), *Der deutsche Bauernkrieg*, in: *Karl Marx. Friedrich Engels. Werke*, vol. 7, Berlin, 327–413.

it proved notably difficult for the peasants to organise themselves into a large-scale revolutionary movement to overthrow the feudal system exploiting them – and, crucially, for them to find allies to take it on, because social fragmentation meant that the needs and interests of any given social group would conflict with those of the peasants and all other groups in society, despite being simultaneously highly interconnected. He believes that it was only as a result of the spread of radical ideas through the Reformation that these groups began to coalesce into a 'Catholic or reactionary' front seeking to preserve religious and secular feudalism and another front seeking to overthrow them, although the latter remained divided into a 'Lutheran bourgeois reforming' camp and a 'revolutionary' camp.

Engels presents Martin Luther and Thomas Müntzer as historical figures who respectively embody the doctrine, character and 'Auftreten' of these oppositional groups. He argues that Luther underwent a process of development between the *95 Theses* in 1517 and the Peasants' War in 1525, the culmination of which is marked by *Wider die Rotten*. He declares that this led to the course of the Reformation increasingly being dictated by the ruling classes and Luther increasingly serving their interests, declaring that "das Volk wußte sehr gut, was es tat, wenn es sagte, er sei ein Fürstendiener geworden wie die andern" (348).

Engels draws attention to its brutality, highlighting several words in quoting Luther with "Man soll sie *zerschmeißen*, *würgen* und *stechen*, *heimlich* und *öffentlich*, wer da kann, wie man einen *tollen Hund* totschlagen muß!" (350). He, like the early modern readers of the Taylorian copies, also picks out the final call to arms with its graphic language: "Darum, liebe Herren, loset hie, rettet da, steche, schlage, würge sie, wer da kann, bleibst du darüber tot, wohl dir, seligeren Tod kannst du nimmer mehr überkommen."

Engels claims that Luther's Bible translation had provided the peasants with a powerful alternative to the existing structures of the medieval Church and society. However, he accuses Luther of turning it against them in his anti-peasant pamphlets, transforming what had once been a tool of revolutionary struggle into a complete "Dithyrambus auf die von Gott eingesetzte Obrigkeit [...] wie ihn kein Tellerlecker der absoluten Monarchie je zustande gebracht hat", disavowing all his previous resistance to the religious and secular feudal authorities, and selling out both the 'bourgeois' and 'plebeian' oppositional movements to the princes.

The other Marxist historical text crucial to GDR interpretations of Luther's anti-peasant pamphlets was *Deutsche Geschichte vom Ausgange des Mittelalters* (1910/11), an outline of German history from the late Middle Ages to the French Revolution based on a series of lectures given at the party college of the Social Democratic Party by the Marxist historian and journalist Franz Mehring (1846–1919).[6] In the introduction, he states that the book is designed to facilitate serious teaching and learning of German history among the wider party membership by not just listing key facts, but attempting to briefly outline the internal logic according to which he sees German history as unfolding, focusing on drawing out a sequence of interconnected historical events that have direct or indirect long-term effects on 'the German workers' movement'. For Mehring, one of the most important events of Early Modern German history is the Peasants' War and the connected Anabaptist movement, in a sub-chapter in which he touches on *Wider die Rotten*. He observes that the peasants initially had a very strong element of surprise on their side during the conflict and appeared to have such a good chance of winning that Luther argued that God himself was rising up against the nobility and advocated for a peaceful settlement based on the demands of the peasants, most of which he considered justified. Mehring mockingly declares that if "bourgeois Protestant" historians were correct in their assessment that the Reformation was shaped by Luther as a great man ra-

---

[6] Mehring, Franz (1964), *Deutsche Geschichte vom Ausgange des Mittelalters*, in: Höhle, Thomas/Koch, Hans/Schleifstein, Josef (edd.), *Franz Mehring. Gesammelte Schriften*, vol. 5: *Zur deutschen Geschichte bis zur Zeit der französischen Revolution 1789*, Berlin.

ther than by social, economic and political change, then his intervention would have changed the course of the conflict. However, he triumphantly proclaims that Luther's intervention did not make the slightest bit of difference. Instead, Mehring uses the pamphlet to portray Luther as a fickle figure who went along with the political wind that prevailed at any given time. He claims that, once the ruling classes had recovered from the initial shock of the uprising and begun preparing to brutally suppress it, Luther abandoned his previous views and 'completely rolled over' ('fiel [...] gänzlich um') by writing *Wider die Rotten*. Mehring emphasised the brutality of Luther's 'bloodthirsty executioner's tone' (*blutdürstiger Henkerston*) and pushing for the 'massacring of the peasants' (*Niedermetzelung der Bauern*).

Wider die Rotten appears first in a source collection published by 'Volk und Wissen Verlag' which provided nearly all textbooks for the GDR. *Zur Geschichte des Großen Deutschen Bauernkrieges: Dokumente und Materialien* (1961) is a reader of sources on the Peasants' War compiled by the Halle historian Walter Zöllner (1932–2011). Since history teachers only had a limited number of lessons allocated to the complex constellations of issues associated with the "early bourgeois revolution", they would need to focus on using primary sources to illustrate the key events of the period, with a focus on "the struggle of the masses of the people". Zöllner includes *Wider die Rotten* in his reader because he regards the pamphlet as a direct response by Luther to this struggle based on his own experience of it.[7]

Zöllner also gives some extracts from the pamphlet based on the text in Volume 18 of the *Weimarer Ausgabe* of Luther's works (1908), preceded by some excerpts from *Eine Ermahnung zum Frieden auf die zwölf Artikeln der Bauern* in modernised spelling.[8] Strikingly, Zöllner omits the entire first section of the pamphlet in which Luther sets out his rationale for writing it, claiming that the peasants had been led

---

[7] Walter Zöllner (1961), *Zur Geschichte des Großen Deutschen Bauernkrieges: Dokumente und Materialien*, Berlin, 3; 15.
[8] Zöllner (1961), 140–42 (*Wider die Rotten*) and 136–40 (*Eine Ermahnung zum Frieden*).

astray by Thomas Müntzer to make false claims in the name of the Gospel in the *Twelve Articles*, and to break their word and do the bidding of the Devil by continuing to escalate the violence.⁹ Crucially, this omission leaves out Luther's statement of intent to make the peasants aware of their sins in the hope that they will recognise themselves and change their ways, enabling Zöllner to present the pamphlet as much more hostile to the peasants from the outset. It also leaves out Luther's declaration of intent to instruct the secular authorities on how to deal with the peasants with a clear conscience, instead beginning with an abridged version of Luther's explanation of the three terrible sins against God and their fellow people that the peasants have committed. This section omits the Bible verses that Luther uses to justify his argument that the peasants have sinned by breaking their vow of obedience and many of Luther's remarks about the Devil. These omissions exemplify the highly secular and materialist approach that historians and literary scholars took to analysing this pamphlet in the GDR, most likely influenced by Engels' arguments in *Der deutsche Bauernkrieg* about the necessity of 'stripping back the veneer of holiness' of Reformation history to reveal and address the 'class struggles' which he saw as underpinning the religious debates of the period.[10]

These extracts are followed by a sub-section containing two documents categorised as 'reactions to Luther'. The first document consists of extracts from a letter by Hermann Mühlpfort, addressee of *Von der Freiheit eines Christenmenschen* (1520) to Master Stephan Roth in Wittenberg. These extracts emphasise what Zöllner describes in his introduction as the hatred for the pamphlet among ordinary people and the heavy criticisms it provoked among Luther's own supporters. The other is an extract from the *Rothenburger Chronik* by Michael Eisenhart. In this extract, Eisenhart claims that Luther had instigated the fighting and the ensuing suffering, but subsequently washed his hands of the responsibility by thoroughly misrepresenting his victims

---

[9] Zöllner, 140.
[10] Engels (1960), 344.

and turning the ruling classes against them, and prays that the same fate would befall Luther himself. This exemplifies Zöllner's claims that Catholic opponents of the Reformation also seized on the pamphlet to accuse Luther of betraying the peasants.

Wider die Rotten der Bauern became the subject of increased interest in the GDR in the years leading up to the commemoration of the 450th anniversary of the Reformation in 1967. For instance, the pamphlet is addressed in *Thomas Müntzer* (1965), an illustrated popular biography of Müntzer by Manfred Bensing (1927–96), then a lecturer in German History in Leipzig and later Professor of the History of the German Workers' Movement and the GDR there from 1969–88.[11] In the foreword, Bensing wishes to show that "Müntzer's short but rich life" was devoted to "the people". Bensing is particularly keen to overcome the distortion of Müntzer's image in *Wider die Rotten*, which he mentions at the conclusion of the section 'Sieg und Niederlage', concerned with the defeat of Müntzer and his allies at the Battle of Frankenhausen on 14 May 1525.[12] Bensing is highly critical of Luther for siding with the princes; describing the peasants' defeat as the victory of God over Satan; accusing Müntzer of leading the people astray; and calling on his readership "to strangle and stab and earn the Kingdom of Heaven with savagery" in the pamphlet – a quotation which was also influential to Engels' characterisation of the pamphlet. This assessment of the brutality encouraged by the pamphlet is underlined by an extract from an image of the woodcut "Die Folter" by Hans Burgkmair the Elder (1473–1531) showing two captured peasants being tortured, which takes up around two thirds of this page in Bensing's biography. In the background, one near-naked peasant is suspended by his wrists from the ceiling of the room with a long rope, with a heavy basket and sacks attached to his ankles and an expression of agony on his face. Three officials around a long table interrogate him, with one pointing accusingly at him and an-

---

[11] Bensing, Manfred (1965), *Thomas Müntzer*, Leipzig.
[12] The following is based on Bensing (1965), 87.

other recording his confession. In the foreground, another near-naked peasant lies flat on his back with his wrists and ankles bound and his neck between two blocks, whilst another figure roughly pulls the peasant's head back by his fringe and forcibly pours liquid into his mouth. Overall, Bensing describes *Wider die Rotten* as "an ugly pamphlet" which represented the "low point" of Luther's pathway "which had begun so promisingly in 1517".

The following year, Bensing returned to this pamphlet in *Thomas Müntzer und der Thüringer Aufstand 1525* (1966), a published version of his 1962 doctoral dissertation on the subject. He groups the pamphlet with other evidence of Luther's participation in the struggle of the feudal reaction against the uprising in Thuringia within a broader chapter on the strategy and tactics of the princes' party and the Thuringian nobility. Bensing declares that Luther's attempt to provide the Protestant princes with 'divine justification' served as "an attempt to retrospectively justify the bloodbath of Frankenhausen and the terrible judgement over the central German movement" – which Bensing argues was also in Luther's own interests because his fortunes would be determined by the outcome of the uprising. Ultimately, despite their lack of influence on contemporary developments, Bensing regards Luther's pamphlets against the Peasants' War as providing a much clearer reflection of his stance on the political events of the time than many of his other writings.[13]

Bensing singles out what he sees as two of many attempts to defend *Wider die Rotten* for criticism. Firstly, he attacks what he sees as the relativisation of the horror of Luther's incitement to violence against the peasants in *Luther: Anbruch und Krise der Neuzeit* (1946, ²1948), by Hanns Lilje (1899–1977), bishop of the *Evangelisch-Lutherische Kirche* in Hanover from 1947–71. Bensing bitterly argues that Luther's claim that rebellious peasants should be killed like mad dogs "verliert [...] an Furchtbarkeit" for Lilje, because he sees Lilje as interpreting this

---

[13] Bensing, Manfred (1966), *Thomas Müntzer und der Thüringer Aufstand 1525*, Berlin, 196ff.

claim to refer only to "wirklich Aufrührer".[14] Lilje had come under sustained attack in the GDR (and was also not uncontroversial in the West) because of his support for NATO and West German re-armament, culminating in a successful GDR campaign to block him from becoming presiding bishop of the *Evangelische Kirche in Deutschland* in 1961.

Additionally, Bensing critiques what he sees as another attempt to justify Luther's arguments against the peasants in this pamphlet by Paul Althaus (1888–1966) in a 1925 article entitled 'Luthers Haltung im Bauernkrieg'. Althaus had been a professor of theology in Erlangen from 1925–47 and 1948–57 and had acquired renown as an expert on Martin Luther, but had also attracted controversy after the Second World War for his support for National Socialism in the early years of the regime, which led to his dismissal as chairman of the university de-nazification commission in Erlangen in 1947. Bensing claims that Althaus regarded Luther's advocacy for the use of violence to suppress the revolt as an inevitable, logical consequence of his interpretation of the social teaching of the Gospel in response to his assessment of the political situation rather than as an expression of personal hostility towards the peasants. Bensing acknowledges that this was a logical consequence of the basic principles of Luther's theology, which he states was particularly focused on questions of authority and obedience. However, he insists that this cannot justify what he regards as Luther's self-interested support for a "bad, anti-humane and anti-progressive" cause in an attempt to preserve the old social and political order on which his teachings depended, making the peasants fair game for attacks whilst denying them the right to punish the ruling classes who Bensing regards as the true 'instigators of the unrest'. Drawing on Kurt Matthes' *Luther und die Obrigkeit* (1937), Bensing describes this discrepancy as a 'loophole' which was highly damaging for Luther's social teaching.[15]

---

[14] Bensing (1966), 198.
[15] Bensing (1966), 197–98.

By criticising these assessments of Luther's pamphlet by a prominent former supporter of National Socialism and a high-profile West German supporter of NATO and re-armament, Bensing stresses the indefensibility of what he regards as Luther's rejection of the 'progressive' cause of the peasants' uprising – and the horrifically violent methods he proposed to suppress it – in the pamphlet by appearing to suggest that they can only be justified from perspectives associated with the 'fascism' of National Socialism or the 'militarism' and 'American imperialism' that the GDR associated with the West and NATO. Because he sees the pamphlets as denying the peasants the right to resist and thereby enshrining their exploitation, Bensing ultimately regards them as documents of betrayal – and their author as a class traitor. He describes the pamphlets as 'betrayal in print'[16] and declares that despite being a 'Bauer- und Bergknappensohn', Luther had nothing in common with the revolutionary-minded townspeople of Wittenberg and the peasants with whom they wished to join forces. Instead, Bensing argues that Luther ended up on the wrong side of 'the great conflicts in society' by switching his allegiance to 'the side of the ruling powers' during the Peasants' War – and suffered the consequences of doing so by becoming their 'tool', whether he liked it or not.[17]

A more nuanced reassessment of Luther as the author of this pamphlet is offered by Gerhard Zschäbitz (1920–70) in *Martin Luther – Größe und Grenze. 1. Teil 1483-1526*, the first instalment of a never-finished two-part biography of Luther published to commemorate the 450th anniversary of the *95 Theses* in 1967. Zschäbitz contends that existing 'bourgeois' Luther scholarship is highly specialist and dominated by perspectives that crowd out enquiry into Luther as an individual living in the society of his time and that Luther anniversary culture often distorted Luther's image for reactionary purposes, especially around the 400th anniversary of the *95 Theses* in 1917. He declares that his biography "is not intended to drape the 'blood-red

---

[16] Bensing (1966), 196.
[17] Bensing (1966), 200.

mantle of the revolutionary' around Luther. It is even less intended to declare Martin Luther a forerunner or fellow-traveller of the SED. We must leave such accusations to the choir of a West German journalist mob." ("[...] will nicht Luther den 'blutroten Mantel des Revolutionärs' umhängen. Noch weniger will es Martin Luther als 'Voroder Mitläufer der SED' deklarieren. Solche Unterstellungen müssen wir dem Chor einer westdeutschen Journaille überlassen.")[18] Instead, he declares that his aim is to make Luther more accessible for his readers in the class struggles of his time.

Zschäbitz argues that the decisive outcome of the Battle of Frankenhausen also represented a decisive outcome for the ongoing conflict between Luther and Müntzer. He declares that Luther produced 'his awful writing' ('seine furchtbare Schrift') 'in a wild rage' ('in wildem Zorne') after the lack of success of his *Ermahnung zum Frieden auf die Zwölf Artikel der Bauern*.[19] Gesturing to Engels' argument that *Wider die Rotten* marks the completion of a period of significant change in Luther's thought between 1517 and 1525, Zschäbitz highlights the apparent contrast between this pamphlet and Luther's writings from just a few years earlier which had so greatly enthused the people. By using the epithet "der große Streiter von Rom"[20] to describe Luther as the author figure of *Wider die Rotten*, Zschäbitz expresses his conviction that the Luther of the early anti-Catholic writings is fundamentally the same as the Luther of *Wider die Rotten*. Boldly challenging Engels' claim that *Wider die Rotten* represents the culmination of a period of an about turn in Luther's attitudes between the *95 Theses* and the Peasants' War, he argues that the pamphlet is a document of the fundamental consistency of Luther's thought in this period, centred around the concept of an immutable world order and the notion

---

[18] Zschäbitz, Gerhard (1967), *Martin Luther – Größe und Grenze. 1. Teil 1483-1526*, Berlin, 7.
[19] Zschäbitz (1967), 202.
[20] Zschäbitz (1967), 204.

that he was living in the last days in which the Devil was sowing chaos before the end of the world.

Instead, Zschäbitz contends that the class struggles that had brought Luther to the top had grown more intense, meaning that he had to choose between the princes and peasants. Faced with such a choice, he naturally sided with the princes due to his position in society as a "son of the bourgeoisie in the service of the princes" ("Bürgerssohn im Fürstendienst"). Zschäbitz sees *Wider die Rotten* and Luther's other interventions in the peasants' war as expressions of the wider mood of his class, which was still managing well within the existing structures of society and feared losing its privileged position in contemporary society to the masses and its property to the numerous other social groups with designs on it. Whilst he concedes that Luther did not do so consciously, he argues that Luther's interventions in the Peasants' War, including *Wider die Rotten*, most closely aligned with the interests of the cautious opposition represented by the educated bourgeoisie.[21]

Nevertheless, Zschäbitz seeks to rehabilitate the pamphlet at least in part by contextualising Luther's attacks as a logical consequence of his position in the contemporary class system. He stresses that such attacks were a consequence of the still underdeveloped nature of the propertied and educated bourgeoisie which recognised the strength of the masses, but was not yet in a position to harness this strength to achieve its own goals. Unsettled by this strength, the only way that the bourgeoisie could respond to it was to turn against its own potential allies. On this basis, Zschäbitz declares that Luther's attacks on the peasants were understandable when viewed in the context of how he had been shaped by the class to which he belonged and the internal logic of his teachings which developed out of this formation. This notably contrasts with Manfred Bensing's bitter attack just the previous year on Paul Althaus' attempt to contextualise the content of the pamphlet as a necessary consequence of the strict logic of Luther's

---

[21] Zschäbitz (1967), 204.

concept of theology. Zschäbitz describes the pamphlet as a particularly regrettable example of how Luther all too frequently abandoned all boundaries in the struggle for his Gospel. However, he roundly rejects narratives around the pamphlet that label Luther as a traitor to the peasants, insisting that he acted in a way that was typical of both his class and time as a bourgeois scholar of his century ("bürgerlicher Gelehrter seines Jahrhunderts").[22] He strikingly revises Engels' claim that the people rightly branded Luther as a 'Fürstendiener', arguing that because the Reformation had lost its impetus as a revolutionary movement following the defeat of the peasants, it needed the support of rulers and their institutions to continue.

Zschäbitz's revisionist view of *Wider die Rotten* and of Luther as its author does not appear to have gained much traction. Instead, traditional perspectives on both dominated by the views of Engels and Mehring appear to have prevailed in the years leading up to the 450th anniversary of the Peasants' Revolt in 1975. An example of this occurs in an edition of *Wider die Rotten* published in 1970 as part of a two-volume edition of selected writings by Ulrich von Hutten, Martin Luther and Thomas Müntzer edited by Siegfried Streller (1921–2015), Professor of German literature at the Humboldt University in East Berlin from 1969–86. Streller selects these three individuals as the most influential and representative writers of the 'early bourgeois revolution' whose thought and actions as author figures are shaped by, and, in turn, shape the events of this period. Drawing on a selection of their writings that he describes as 'Kampfschriften' and 'agitatorische Schriften', he declares that they stand out from later works of high literature because they are based on an understanding of literature as a means of influencing the debates in society ("ein Mittel [...] mit dem auf die gesellschaftlichen Auseinandersetzungen gewirkt wird").[23] He also argues that, to achieve this objective, all three address the radical social change of their day in a particularly

---

[22] Zschäbitz (1967), 208.
[23] Streller, Siegfried (1970), *Hutten. Müntzer. Luther. Werke in zwei Bänden*, Berlin/Weimar, v.

stirring way which enriches German language and literature with new forms of expression that become important for their later development, rendering their writings of particular interest as documents of literary aesthetics as well as historical events.

Streller situates Luther's pamphlets against the Peasants War among his most important 'Kampfschriften' of the period opposing radical attempts to reshape society and promoting obedience to authority. For Streller, with his arguments in *Wider die Rotten*, Luther unconditionally went over to the side of the ruling classes ("trat [...] bedingungslos auf die Seite der Herrschenden"), prioritising the interests of the ruling classes over the fight against the teachings of the Church. He claims that, with this pamphlet, Luther lost the respect and support of the masses and effectively placed the future of the Reformation in the hands of the princes, leading it to lose its power as a mass movement and shift its focus to codifying its teaching and protecting it against perceived threats from other anti-papal movements such as the Anabaptists and Zwinglians. He also sees it as a crucial step on what he regards as Luther's journey from thinking like a 'Besitzbürger' to ultimately joining the ranks of the bourgeoisie by getting married and taking a leading role in state-sponsored expressions of the Reformation. Despite its irrelevance to the immediate outcome of the Peasants' War, Streller asserts that *Wider die Rotten* had much longer-term consequences for the conflict, arguing that the pamphlet contributed to creating a distorted image ('Zerrbild') of this significant revolutionary uprising ("diese bedeutende revolutionäre Erhebung") that would go down in German history.[24]

A further move away from Zschäbitz' revisionist interpretation of *Wider die Rotten* can be observed in Max Steinmetz's *Das Müntzerbild von Martin Luther bis Friedrich Engels* (1971), a study of the representation and reception of Thomas Müntzer from Luther to Engels. Max Steinmetz (1912-90) was Professor of History in Leipzig from 1960-

---

[24] Streller (1970), xxxii–xxxiii.

77 and one of the GDR's most influential historians of the Reformation and Peasants' War. In this study, Steinmetz draws on Manfred Bensing's interpretation of *Wider die Rotten* as a reckoning with Thomas Müntzer, moving away from Zschäbitz' attempt to contextualise the pamphlet as typical of the attitudes of Luther's class and instead presenting it as an hysterical, self-interested attempt on Luther's part to discredit him. For Steinmetz, Luther was acutely aware of the gulf emerging between him and the people, and of how much Müntzer had filled this vacuum and become an opponent to be reckoned with. He suggests that this realisation had led Luther to become carried away by the highly emotive nature of the fight against Müntzer, such that he finally had given free vent to his hate, describing *Wider die Rotten* as a "Pamphlet, das an Härte und Grausamkeit nicht mehr zu übertreffen war".[25] Steinmetz argues that the much harder line that Luther took against Müntzer in *Wider die Rotten* – no longer using humour against him, but instead making him the direct target of pure hatred – would set the tone for Luther's remaining attacks on him in *Eine schreckliche Geschichte und Gericht Gottes über Thomas Müntzer* and the *Sendbrief von dem harten Büchlein wider die Bauern*.[26]

A new scholarly edition of the pamphlet was produced in 1975 as part of *Flugschriften der Bauernkriegszeit*, a volume of editions of pamphlets from the Peasants' War marking the 450th anniversary of the conflict. The editors situate the pamphlet among a series of others which they see as documenting the stance of the moderate bourgeois camp towards the revolutionary popular movement. They suggest that pamphlets gathered in this section reveal a diverse range of attitudes towards the peasants' movement among bourgeois Lutherans, including what they perceive as particularly striking differences between the attitudes of the Wittenberg Reformers around Martin Luther and the reformers in the southern German-speaking lands. They

---

[25] Steinmetz, Max (1971), *Das Müntzerbild von Martin Luther bis Friedrich Engels*, Berlin, 19.

[26] Steinmetz (1971), 19 /22.

argue that some of the Reformers were more sympathetic to the cause of the peasants. For instance, they present Nikolaus Herman's pamphlet *Mandat Jesu Christi* as an appeal to fight against the old powers, if only with the weapons of the Gospel, and highlight that other reformers were not as outspoken as Luther in their condemnation of it because they possessed greater understanding of the social issues affecting 'the people'.[27]

In contrast to these more compassionate and socially conscious attitudes, the editors declare that the pamphlet takes Luther's rejection of 'the people' as an active participant in society in his 'propaganda' promoting the Treaty of Weinhausen to an entirely new level. They argue that the pamphlet was used to retrospectively justify the crushing of the revolt at the Battle of Frankenhausen (which, like Bensing, they dub 'the bloodbath of Frankenhausen' because of the peasant losses). They compare Luther's pamphlet and a similarly strident one with appeals for calm by two South German Reformers alarmed by the violence with which the revolt was suppressed, suggesting that such Reformers possessed a much more nuanced understanding of the needs of the people and the responsibilities of the authorities than Luther, and feared that the Reformation would come to share the same fate as the peasants. Furthermore, they contrast these perspectives with a glimpse of more moderate responses to the situation in Bavaria, which managed to avoid most of the fighting despite the equal intensity of the political situation there.[28]

A final shift in attitudes towards *Wider die Rotten* occurred around the time of the commemorations of the quincentenary of the birth of Martin Luther in 1983. A striking example of this change can be observed in the treatment of Luther's pamphlets on the Peasants' War in *Martin Luther. Dokumente seines Lebens und Wirkens* (1983), a commemorative coffee-table book giving an account of Luther's life and

---

[27] *Flugschriften der Bauernkriegszeit* (1975), ed. Adolf Laube and Hans Werner Seiffert, Berlin, 273.
[28] *Flugschriften der Bauernkriegszeit* (1975), 274–75.

times based on pamphlets and other related documents held in GDR libraries and archives. The volume addresses *Wider die Rotten* together with Luther's earlier pamphlet *Eine Ermahnung zum Frieden* on a single page, accompanied by black-and-white images of the titlepage of a copy of each pamphlet held in the *Staatliche Lutherhalle* in Wittenberg, and a short scholarly bibliography on the pamphlets at the end of the book with relevant secondary literature on both listed under *Eine Ermahnung zum Frieden*.

This volume reveals that the pamphlet and its calls for the bloody suppression of the Peasants' War remained a highly uncomfortable document for GDR historians that created strong tensions with the official image of Luther that they were tasked with projecting. The editors attempt to mitigate previous unfavourable assessments of *Wider die Rotten* by presenting it as consistent with Luther's wider approach to public discourse and the attitudes of his contemporaries in Wittenberg. They contextualise Luther's warning to the peasants not to use violence against their rulers in *Eine Ermahnung zum Frieden* as a logical consequence of his concept of obedience and his limited objectives centred around those of the secular rulers. However, they sum up the message of *Wider die Rotten* as an appeal for the annihilation of all rebels ("Aufruf zur Vernichtung aller Aufständischen")[29] which not only oversteps the boundaries of propriety in public discourse as Zschäbitz earlier acknowledged, but, more importantly, also oversteps the boundaries of the internal logic governing Luther's thought and actions and cannot be justified by them. Furthermore, the editors draw attention to the outrage and dismay of some of Luther's contemporaries in response to the pamphlet (particularly Hermann Mühlpfort in his letter to Stephan Roth frequently cited in previous GDR literature on it, and, drawing on *Flugschriften der Bauernkriegzeit*, the South German Reformers), forcing him to publicly respond by calling for an end to the bloodshed he had earlier

---

[29] *Martin Luther. Dokumente seines Lebens und Wirkens* (1983), Weimar, 156.

promoted, even if he continued to justify the suppression of the revolt by the authorities.

Overall, GDR interpreters were united in their distaste for and condemnation of the pamphlet's tone and content, almost universally considering it an angry and hateful text characterised by brutality and bloodlust. They also consistently regarded it as unsuccessful in its objective of convincing the nobility to act against the peasants, but later used to great effect to retrospectively justify the atrocities involved in suppressing the revolt and decisively turn popular memory of the conflict against the peasants. Around the 1967 Reformation anniversary, Gerhard Zschäbitz developed a striking revisionist assessment of the pamphlet that sought to rehabilitate Luther as the author of *Wider die Rotten* by contextualising the pamphlet as a product of Luther's middle-class origins and arguing that it demonstrated much greater consistency with his earlier theology and thought than had been previously acknowledged. However, this interpretation does not appear to have caught on, and a return to more traditional views of the pamphlet more heavily influenced by Marx and Engels dominated its reception until the commemorations of the 450th anniversary of the Peasants' War in 1975.

Around the 500th anniversary of Martin Luther's birth in 1983, GDR interpreters made further but less far-reaching attempts to revise interpretations of the pamphlet. They softened their language around the pamphlet and argued that its sentiments were far from unique to Luther, but this time made no attempt to contextualise it within his class background or theological system, presenting it as an extreme pamphlet that overstepped the mark in all respects. This highlights the astonishingly long-lasting impact of Luther's pamphlets against the Peasants' War edited in this volume, which continued to provoke strong reactions and shape ideological assessments of him four and a half centuries after their publication.

3. The Pamphlets in Oxford
Henrike Lähnemann

The Peasants' War intensified the pamphlet war and led to an even more increased output of publications. This is evident in the fact that every pamphlet by Martin Luther on the topic exists in multiple editions in both the Taylorian and Bodleian Libraries. The following bibliographical survey highlights some of the book-historical features of the Oxford copies, particularly where they show how contemporary readers engaged with the text.

The Taylorian copies were mainly bought in 1878, among them 139 duplicates from Heidelberg University Library, acquired via London bookseller David Nutt in December for a total price of £25, by Heinrich Krebs for Professor Friedrich Max Müller (all shelfmarks with Arch.G.8°1525).[1] The Bodleian copies came to the library from Sotheby's as preconfigured *Sammelbände* in 1818. The previous German owner, an Augsburg librarian, had arranged to bind pamphlets from the same year adjacent to each other. Therefore, most of the Peasants' War pamphlets are concentrated in a couple of volumes from the 'Tractatus Lutherani' (Tr.Luth.).[2]

---

[1] Oxford, Oxford University Archives – Taylor Institution, TL 3/2/3: Registers of additions to the Library (accession registers). 1877–82. More on this in the bibliographical section of previous Reformation pamphlets, particularly the essay by Maximilian Krümpelmann (2020) 'The History of the Taylorian Copies' in vol. 3 *Von der Freiheit eines Christenmenschen*, also the catalogue *German in the World* (2025). Forthcoming: Christina Ostermann and Henrike Lähnemann, 'Friedrich Max Müller and the Acquisition of Reformation Pamphlets at the Taylor Institution Library', in: *Migration Collections: Translocation Research in Libraries and Archives, 1850–2025*. Special Issue of the *Forum for Modern Language Studies*, ed. Sophia Buck and Stefanie Hundehege.

[2] On the collection history of the series see also previous volumes of Reformation pamphlets, particularly the essay by Philip Flacke (2024) 'The Pamphlets in Oxford' in vol. 7 *Hans Sachs*.

lxxiv The Pamphlets

1. *Ermahnung zum Frieden*

The first pamphlet – and mildest in tone – is the 'Admonition to Peace' as answer to the 12 articles of the peasants, issued in April. The Taylorian has two and the Bodleian no fewer than five different editions. While none of the printers of Peasants' War pamphlets revealed their name or the place of publication, it is clear from title border and typeface that the first edition was printed in Wittenberg by Josef Klug. The copy in the Taylorian (1) belongs to an early print run since the frame at the bottom of the page is still empty, while in later copies, Psalm 7:16 in Latin was added. In the second edition in the Bodleian (2), the psalm verse is in German, which also later appears on the next Peasants' War pamphlet (see the edition below).

> 1. ARCH.8°.G.1525(11): *Ermanunge zum | fride auff die zwelff | artikel der Bawr- | schafft ynn | Schwaben. | Mart. Luther | Wittemberg | 1525.* [Wittenberg: Josef Klug,] 1525. [20] fols; 4° VD16 L 4690.

Wittenberg: (1) Taylorian, ARCH.8°.G.1525(11) / (2) Bodleian, Tr. Luth. 98(4)
Early print run of the 1st edition with empty border / 2nd edition with Psalm 7:16

2. Tr. Luth. 98(4): *Ermanunge zum | fride auff die zwelff artickel | der Bawrschafft ynn | Schwaben. | Auch widder die reubischen | vnd mordisschen rotten | der andern bawren. | Mart. Luther.* [Wittenberg: Josef Klug,] 1525. VD16 L 4692.

Klug prominently integrated into his title woodcut the 'Lutherrose', Luther's seal of authorisation consisting of a cross in a heart surrounded by rose petals, developed in 1524 to protect Luther's texts (and Wittenberg printers) from unauthorized copyists. This seal is conspicuously missing in the third copy with the same title frame (3), and even if the 'Wittemberg' in the bottom frame (rather than directly following Luther's name) probably tried to make it look like it had been printed there, it was actually produced in Augsburg.

3. Tr. Luth. 41(26): *Ermanunge | zum Fryde/ auff die | zwölff Artickel der | Bawrschafft | in Schwa=|ben. | Mar. Lut. || Wittemberg. M.D.xxv.* [Augsburg: Philipp Ulhart,] 1525. VD16 L 4678.

Augsburg: (3) Tr. Luth. 41(27)
Luther's authorisation seal has been replaced by an empty shield

Tübingen: (4) Tr. Luth. 98(13)
The woodcut with a plethora of fantastical beasts such as elephants, camels and a gigantic bird among half-clad puttos is dated 1519. It had clearly been in heavy use up to this 1525 edition, as the broken border and other missing elements show.

in Oxford lxxvii

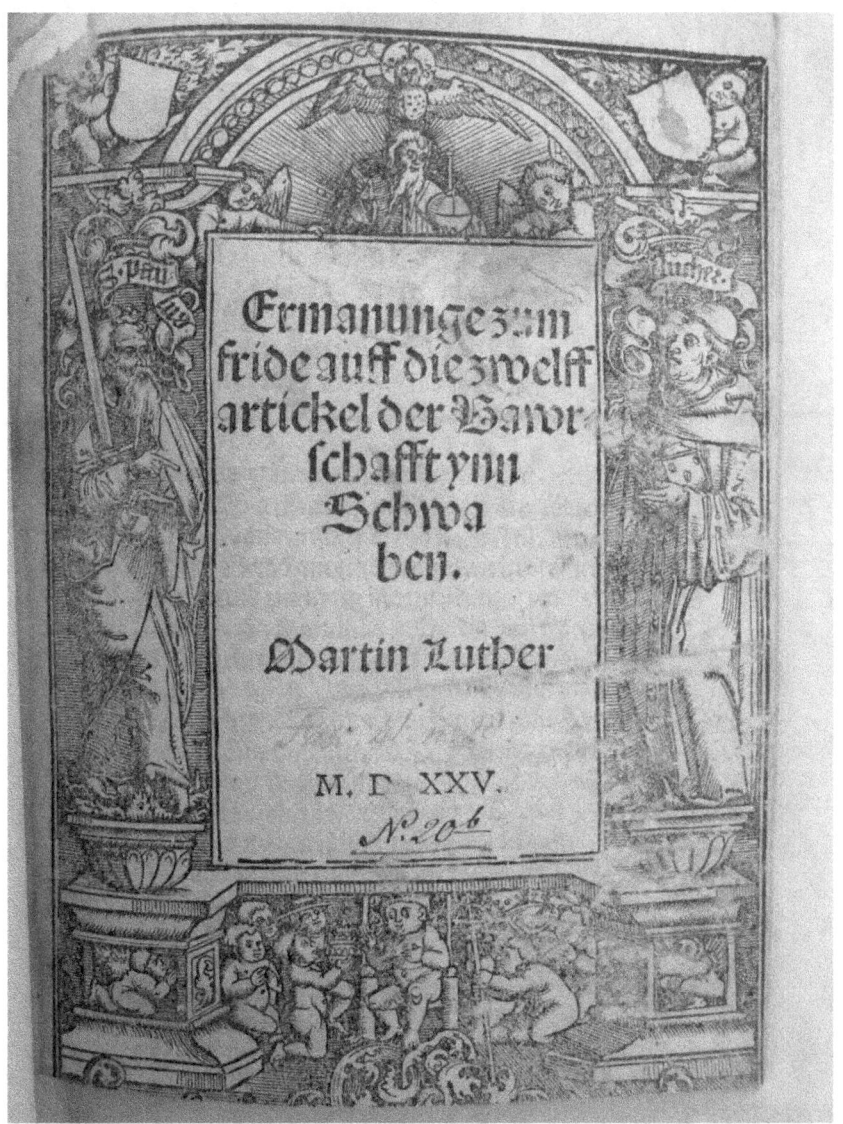

Strasbourg: (5) Tr. Luth. 41(28)
'S. Paulus' and 'Luther' are featured with their names on the scroll to both sides of the title; below, a group of cherubs, one with a cardinal's hat on, another with a mitre, are offering a tiara to the cherub on a throne in the middle.

Augsburg: (6) Tr. Luth. 41(27)
Top: baptism of Christ. Sides: scenes from the Acts of the Apostles
(Philip baptises the eunuch, Paul at Damascus, Peter's dream, Paul on Malta)
below a figure with a quotation from Juvenal, *Satires*, 1.160: *digito conpesce labellum*
(with your finger button your lip) and the printer's mark showing Hercules

4. Tr. Luth. 98(13): *Ermanunge zum | frid/ auff die zwölff Arti=|ckel der Bawrschafft | in Schwaben. | Mar. Lut. || Wittemberg. M.D.xxv.* [Tübingen: Ulrich Morhart,] 1525. VD16 L 4689.

5. Tr. Luth. 41(28): *Ermanunge zum | fride auff die zwelff | artickel der Bawr= | schafft ynn | Schwa | ben. | Martin Luther.* [Strasbourg: Wolfgang Köpfel,] 1525. VD16 L 4687.

6. Tr. Luth. 41(27): *Ermanung zům | frid/ auf die zwölf | artickel d' baur | schafft ynn | Schwa | ben. Martinus Luther.* [Augsburg: Simprecht Ruff,] 1525. VD16 L 4677.

The Taylorian copy of the Nuremberg edition (7) has been heavily thumbed, with torn off corners; the marginal comments of one contemporary reader have been mostly washed off, while another early reader used the empty space in the central frame for pen trials; obviously, this copy has passed through many hands. The same reader seems also seems to have scribbled on the Nuremberg edition of *Wider die Rotten* (see the copy 2 in chapter 3.2 and the facsimile in the appendix). Pamphlets were often first read in the city where they were printed and then bound together to make the ephemeral publications fit for shelving as books. Since both editions also show tears on the side of the page where presumably originally a tab was glued on. This points to their previous co-existence in a *Sammelband* before they were separated again for sale, then picked up by the Taylorian librarian Heinrich Krebs for the Reformation project of Friedrich Max Müller in 1878 and bound as single items with empty pages added in for scholarly note-taking.

7. ARCH.8°.G.1525(10): *Ermanunge zum | fride / auff die zwelff | Artickel der Pawr- | schafft in Swaben. | Martinus Luther | Wittemberg | 1525* [Nuremberg: Jobst Gutknecht,] 1525. [14] fols; 4° VD16 L 4684.

Nuremberg: (4) ARCH.8°.G.1525(10)
Pen trials probably by the same reader as the Nuremberg edition of *Wider die Rotten* ARCH.8°.G.1525(27). There are barely legible German marginalia, e.g. at the bottom of the titlepage which somebody, probably a book dealer in the 19th century, tried to wash off, starting with *wenn ich*…

2. *Wider die Rotten der Bauern*

The second pamphlet, which is the one edited in this volume, was originally drafted as an addendum to the *Ermahnung* (see chapter 3.1) but soon took on a life of its own. The longer title of the Erfurt edition (2) reflects this publication history. All other editions adapt the title to the actual content of the short treatise which only fills one quire in quarto. The psalm verse, which was later added to the titlepage of the *Ermahnung* in Latin has been integrated into the running title in German. For further discussion of the change in title and details of the ironic marginalia and the underlining in both editions of some of the starkest sentences of the pamphlet see chapter 1.1 and the facsimile. All editions comprise just four folios in quarto format.

None of the editions has a publication place or printer's name, reflecting the contentious tone of the pamphlet; the identity of the publishers had to be established by comparing the typefaces with signed editions. The Nuremberg edition is set in the same typeface as editions by Friedrich Peypus whose printer's device was a coat of arms showing mugwort – 'Beifuß' in German, cognate to Peypus.

Peypus' printer's device on the titlepage / 15v of ARCH.8°.G.1520(19)
Ein Sermon von dem newen Testament, Nuremberg 1520, VD16 L 6405

lxxxii *The Pamphlets*

1. ARCH.8°.G.1525(27): *Wider die mor|dischen vnd reubischen | Rotten der Pawren. | Martinus Luther. | Wittemberg.* [Nuremberg: Friedrich Peypus,] 1525. VD16 L 7494

2. ARCH.8°.G.1525(28): *Wider die sturmē-|den Bawren | Auch wider die reu | bischen vnd mȯrdisschen rottē | der andern Bawren. | Marti. Luther | Wittemberg.* [Erfurt: Matthäus Maler,] 1525. VD16 L 7482

The title woodcut of the Erfurt edition, produced by Matthäus Maler in a small workshop which reprinted successful Protestant pamphlets such as the 'Passional Christi und Antichristi' ARCH.8o.G.1521(19), is particularly incongruous with the content, showing playing putti. The date on the shield of the trumpet-blowing angel marks this as a copy of an older woodcut, since it shows the date '1521' in reverse.

(2) ARCH.8°.G.1525(28) – for the full titlepage see the facsimile at the end
The trumpet angel with the year inverted / mirrored to show the original model

There are three copies of the pamphlet in the Bodleian:

3. Tr. Luth. 98(14): *WJder die mördischē | vnnd reubischenn | Rottenn der Paurenn. | Martinus Lutther. | Wittemberg.* [Bamberg: Georg Erlinger, 1525]. VD16 L 7479

4. Tr. Luth. 98(23): *Wider die Mordischen vn͂ | Reubischen Rotten | der Bawren: | Martinus Luther: | Wittemberg* [Augsburg: Heinrich Steiner,] 1525. VD16 L 7477 [not on SOLO]

5. Tr. Luth. 41(22): *Wider die mordischen | vnd Reubischen Rot=|ten der Pawren. | Martinus Luther. | Wittemberg* [Nuremberg: Jobst Gutknecht, 1525]. VD16 L 7493

(5) Tr. Luth. 41(22) The Nuremberg edition by Jobst Gutknecht which imitates the coat of arms of Wittenberg on the top border and shows the whore of Babylon on the seven-headed dragon from the Book of Revelation at the bottom

3. *Sendbrief von dem harten Büchlein wider die Bauern*

The last pamphlet, originally meant as an apology or at least an explanation of Luther's take on the issue, turned into an even more vicious confirmation of his condemnation, see chapter 1.1. Again, none of the printers displayed their name or the place of publication in this much longer treatise, but all of them highlight the publication year on the titlepage to advertise to potential buyers that this is brand-new material. The Augsburg edition also announces the conclusion added by Urbanus Rhegius (1489–1541), a Protestant Reformer who took a more nuanced position on the plight of the peasants and tried to moderate Luther's extreme stance.

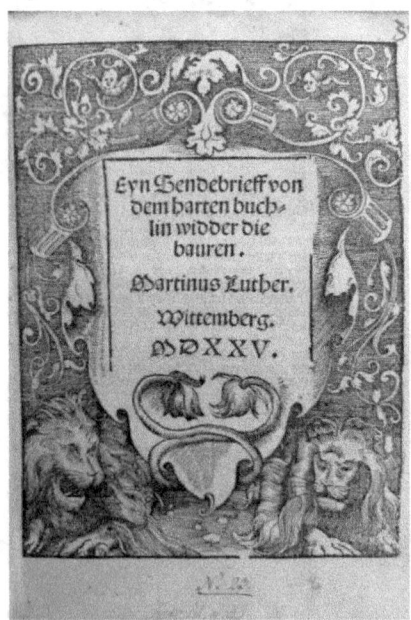 

(1) ARCH.8°.G.1525(14/1) / (2) ARCH.8°.G.1525(14/2)
The stock borders show lions (1) and a mix of classical scenes (2).

The pamphlet comprises between 12 and 16 folios, i.e. between three and four large sheets folded into quarto quires, depending on the typeface. None of the Oxford copies show the signs of wear and tear which are noticeable in the earlier, shorter and punchier pamphlets.

1. ARCH.8°.G.1525(14/1): *Eyn Sendebrieff von | dem harten buch- | lin widder die | bauren. | Martinus Luther. | Wittemberg. | MDXXV.* [Wittenberg: Michael Lotter,] 1525. [16] fols; VD16 L 5944. Bound with (2)

2. ARCH.8°.G.1525(14/2): *Ain Sendbrieff von dem | hartē büchlin wider | die bauren. | Martinus Luther. | Schlußred D. Vrba-|ni Regii / vom weltlichen ge-|walt wider die auff- | rürischen.* [Augsburg: Simprecht Ruff,] 1525. [14] fols; VD16 L 5938

3. Tr. Luth. 41(34): same edition as (2)

4. Tr. Luth. 41(33)[3]: *Eyn Sendebrieff von | dem harten buch=|lin widder die | bauren. | Martinus Luther. | Wittemberg* [Wittenberg: Michael Lotter,] 1525. VD16 L 5944

5. ARCH.8°.G.1525(15): *Eyn Sendebrieff | von dem harten büch | lin wider die | Bawrn | M. Luther. | 1525.* [Nuremberg: Hans Hergot,] 1525. [12] fols; VD16 L 5942

Luther wrote to the town council in Nuremberg in 1525 accusing Hans Hergot (the 'Herrgöttlein') of unauthorised reprinting of his texts. Hergot belonged to a more radical side of the Reformation and was executed in Leipzig in 1527 for a pamphlet in which he developed socialist utopian ideas. His widow Kunigunde continued the workshop in Nuremberg until 1538.

---

[3] This edition is not catalogued on SOLO which lists only 32 pamphlets under Tr. Luth. 41.

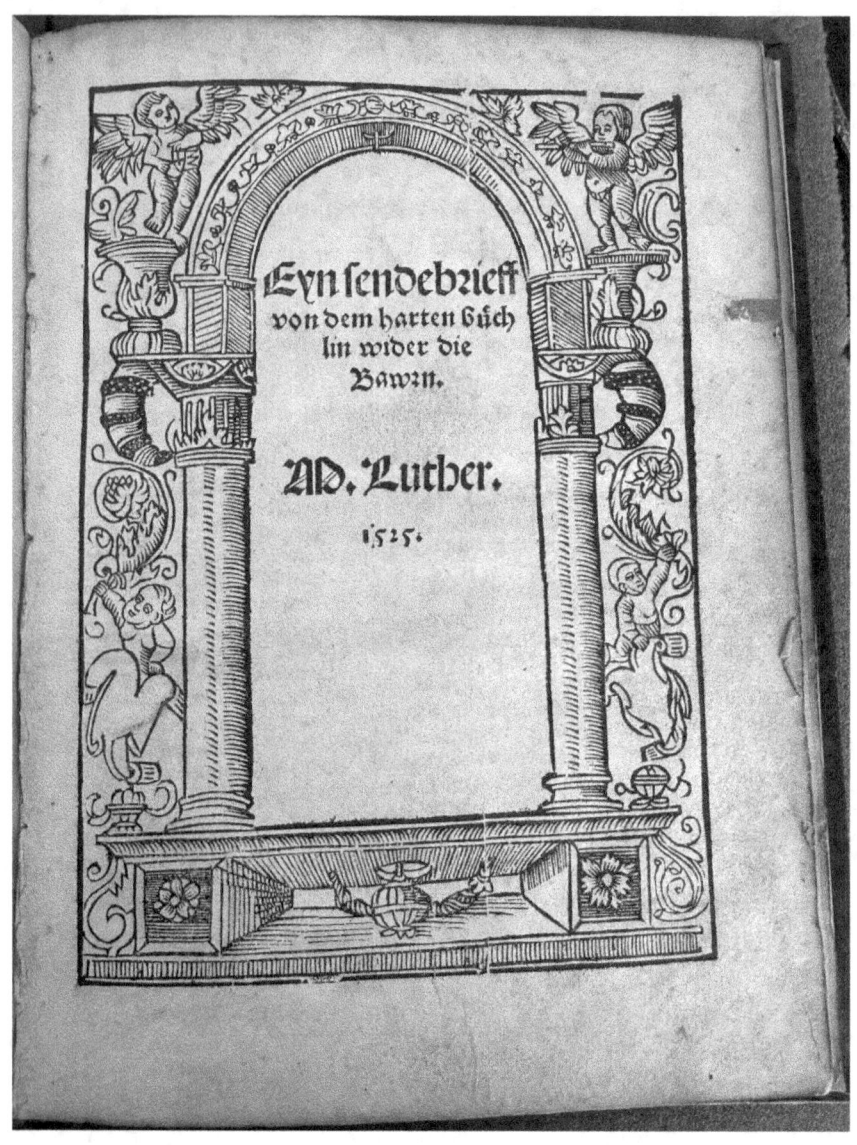

ARCH.8°.G.1525(15), the edition by the 'Herrgöttlein'
As with many of the other Peasants' War pamphlets, the title borders is taken from the stock images of the print workshop, in this case with cherubs making a joyous noise with bells and whistles particularly incongruous to the content.

4. Introduction to the Edition

Martin Luther's *Wider die Rotten der Bauern* is written as a vicious call to action, to be performed as inflammatory speech filled with rolling cadences, alliterations, and repetitions which hammer home the message of the pamphlet. To appreciate the intended impact of this, it is therefore best to read this pamphlet out aloud – an advice which has been holding true also for other pamphlets in the series, particularly the *Sendbrief vom Dolmetschen* with its argument for idiomatic German and for Hans Sachs' Reformation dialogues.

1. Punctuation
   Early modern editions use full stops, brackets, question marks, and virgules as punctuation marks. The '/' Virgel (virgule or forward slash) is the main means of structuring sentences and can stand for both a comma and a semicolon. It is best to treat a virgule like a musical caesura, to pause for breath. Often the full stop at the end of a sentence is omitted, particularly if a capital letter follows and conversely a sentence can go on after what looks like a full stop.

2. Abbreviations
   Typesetters took over from manuscripts some handy ways to save space. The main abbreviation mark is a bar (macron) over characters '-'. As a nasal bar above any letter, it replaces a following n such as *deñ* = 'denn' or (rarer in German) an m such as *zū* = 'zum'. The macron is also habitually used for *vñ* = 'und'. In this short German pamphlet, neither of the printers of the Taylorian copies uses any rarer form of abbreviation, either because their font did not include them or they were not necessary for this text which did not quite fill the eight pages of a quarto quire.

3. u/v/w – v/f – i/j/y, and different s– and r–forms
   The Roman alphabet had only one symbol for u and v and one for i and j. u/v/w are interchangeable, as are i/j/y, and v/f are both used for f, e.g. *vrteylen* = 'urteilen', *fewr* = 'feur'. In

lxxxviii *Introduction*

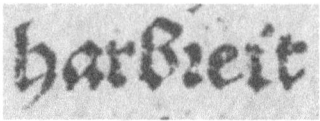

harbreit with the two r forms

most cases, letters are pronounced as in the equivalent modern German word.

The two typographically different forms for s (long ſ versus round s) and for r (the round form of r = ꝛ being mainly used after characters with a rounded right-hand border such as o or – in some fonts – h) in the type set have not been distinguished in the transcription because they are simply graphic variations.

4. Umlauts
   The umlaut sound would have been in the same position as in modern German, but there is no strict rule for writing it. In most cases, an umlaut should be used wherever one occurs in modern German. The Nuremberg print workshop used superscript 'e' for 'ö' and 'ü', 'e' for 'ä'.

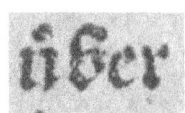

über with a superscript *e* for 'über'

5. Double versus single consonants and s/ß, k/ck, z/tz, r/rh, t/th
   There is no consistency in writing single and double consonants such as f/ff or n/nn, nor is there a difference in pronunciation, i.e. *leutte* and *leute* are pronounced the same. This also applies to s and ß (the latter started out as a ligature of long ſ and z to indicate a double consonant), to k and ck (the spelling for double k), and to z and tz, although there is a tendency in the pamphlet to use 'ß' at the end of words and 'ss' in the middle. Note that z always sounds like modern German z, i.e. /ts/, not like English z. Again, almost all consonants can be pronounced like their modern German equivalents.

6. Use of h and e after vowels; long and short vowels
   While in medieval German each letter would have been

sounded, e.g. 'lieb' would have had a diphthong in the middle, 'e' after other vowels had become silent in the sixteenth century. This is evident from the use of e after i where there never was a diphthong, e.g. the word 'sie'. The same applies to h. In most instances a following e or h indicates a long preceding vowel, but this is not consistent, e.g. 'jm' can stand both for modern *im* and *ihm*. Do not therefore pronounce h and e after vowels, but use long vowels as in modern German.

7. Word division and 'Zusammenschreibung'
   Hyphens in the form of '=' are used frequently but not consistently to indicate the continuation of words across linebreaks; if typesetters ran out of space in a line, they would assume that the reader would be able to link words without this visual prompt. Clear single words have been joined in the transcription but the irregular use of spaces between compounds has not been normalized.

8. Capital letters
   Capital letters are used as in English to indicate the beginning of new sentences and for proper names but also for emphasis in words; these have not been normalized since they can be used for highlighting key terms.

9. Syncope, apocope, and contraction
   Unstressed vowels are often absent where we should expect them in NHG; this is particularly pronounced in Upper German dialects, either mid-word (syncope), or at word-end (apocope). Vowel loss also occurs by contraction.

The Nuremberg edition which has been used as basis for this edition uses only few characteristic features of the region such as 'pawren' for NHG 'Bauern' since the city's printers tried to reach as wide an audience as possible since people from all over Germany.

5. Bibliography

The bibliography is a combination of full references for short titles used in the footnotes of the introduction and some general introductory books. This is obviously not exhaustive and is designed mainly for anglophone students of history and German historical linguistics.

1. Abbreviations

DWb. – *Deutsches Wörterbuch*. https://woerterbuchnetz.de/?sigle=DWB. References 's.v.' (sub voce) reference the lemma which is explained.
Fnhd. Wb. – *Frühneuhochdeutsches Wörterbuch*. https://fwb-online.de/.
KJV – *The Holy Bible, Conteyning the Old Testament, and the New: Newly Translated out of the Originall tongues: & with the former Translations diligently compared and reuised, by his Maiesties speciall Comandement*. London: Robert Barker 1611. Open Access Version on biblija.net.
L45 – Martin Luther: *Biblia: das ist: Die gantze Heilige Schrifft: Deudsch Auffs new zugericht. D.Mart.Luth.* Wittemberg: Hans Lufft 1545. Open Access Version on biblija.net.
VD 16 – *Verzeichnis der im deutschen Sprachbereich erschienenen Drucke des 16. Jahrhunderts*. Open Access (Full bibliographic reference for all Reformation pamphlets with linked-in digitized copies, continually updated; links: http://gateway-bayern.de/VD16+[letter]+[number]).
WA – *Martin Luther: Werke. Kritische Gesamtausgabe [Weimarer Ausgabe]*. Weimar 1883 ff.
VLC – *Vulgata Clementina, 1592. Biblia Sacra juxta Vulgatam Clementinam*. M. Tweedale (ed.). http://vulsearch.sourceforge.net/html, accessed via biblija.net – the Bible on the Internet. Biblical books are given with the abbreviations used for the Vulgate.

2. Secondary Literature

Appold, Kenneth G. (2025): Luther and the Peasants: Religion, Ritual, and the Revolt of 1525, Oxford.
Attar, Karen (ed.) (^{3}2016): *Directory of Rare Book and Special Collections in the UK and Republic of Ireland*. London: Facet.
Bagchi, David (2016): 'Printing, Propaganda, and Public Opinion in the Age of Martin Luther' in *Oxford Research Encyclopedia of Religion*. Oxford: OUP. Open Access.

Bensing, Manfred (1965), *Thomas Müntzer*, Leipzig.
Bensing, Manfred (1966), *Thomas Müntzer und der Thüringer Aufstand 1525*, Berlin.
Bierbrauer, Peter (1980): 'Bäuerliche Revolten im Alten Reich. Ein Forschungsbericht', in: *Aufruhr und Empörung? Studien zum bäuerlichen Widerstand im Alten Reich*, ed. Peter Blickle, Peter Bierbrauer, Renate Blickle, and Claudia Ulbrich, Munich, 1-68
Bischoff, Georges (2010): *La guerre des Paysans: L'alsace et la révolution du Bundschuh 1493-1525*, Strasbourg.
Blickle, Peter (1986): 'The Criminalization of Peasant Resistance in the Holy Roman Empire: Toward a History of the Emergence of High Treason in Germany', *The Journal of Modern History* 58, Supplement (Dec.): Politics and Society in the Holy Roman Empire, 1500-1806.
Brecht, Martin (1989): 'Thomas Müntzers Christologie', in: *Der Theologe Thomas Müntzer. Untersuchungen zu seiner Entwicklung und Lehre;* ed. by Siegfried Bräuer and Helmar Junghans, Berlin, 62–83.
Bräuer, Siegfried and Helmar Junghans (eds.) (1989), *Der Theologe Thomas Müntzer. Untersuchungen zu seiner Entwicklung und Lehre*, Berlin.
Creasman, Allyson F. (2012): *Censorship and Civic Order in Reformation Germany,1517–1648: 'Printed Poison & Evil Talk'*. London / New York: Routledge.
Der Bundschuh. Die Erhebungen des Südwestdeutschen Bauernstandes in den Jahren 1493-1517 (1927), vol. 2: Quellen, ed. Albert Rosenkranz, Heidelberg, no. 21, 110-11.
Der deutsche Bauernkrieg, Aktenband (1935), ed. Günther Franz, Munich.
Drummond, Andrew (2024): *The Dreadful History and Judgement of God on Thomas Müntzer: The Life and Times of an Early German Revolutionary*. London/New York: Verso.
Engels, Friedrich (1960): *Der deutsche Bauernkrieg*, in: *Karl Marx. Friedrich Engels. Werke*, vol. 7, Berlin, 327–413.
Franz, Günther (1933): *Der deutsche Bauernkrieg*, Munich / Berlin.
Ghiselli, Anja, Kari Kopperi and Rainer Vinke (eds.) (1993), *Luther und Ontologie. Das Sein im Glauben als strukturierendes Prinzip der Theologie Luthers*, Helsinki/Erlangen.
Goertz, Hans-Jürgen (1980): *Die Täufer. Geschichte und Deutung*, München.
Goertz, Hans-Jürgen (1989): 'Zu Thomas Müntzers Geistverständnis', in: *Der Theologe Thomas Müntzer. Untersuchungen zu seiner Entwicklung und Lehre;* ed. by Siegfried Bräuer and Helmar Junghans, Berlin, 84–99.

Goertz, Hans-Jürgen (2015): *Thomas Müntzer. Revolutionär am Ende der Zeiten*, München.
Gritsch, Eric W. (1989): 'Thomas Müntzers Glaubensverständnis', in: *Der Theologe Thomas Müntzer. Untersuchungen zu seiner Entwicklung und Lehre;* ed. by Siegfried Bräuer and Helmar Junghans, Berlin, 156–73.
Habermas, J. (²1997): *Theorie des kommunikativen Handelns*, vol. 1, Frankfurt a. M.
Kaufmann, Thomas (2019): *Die Mitte der Reformation*. Tübingen.
Kaufmann, Thomas (2019b): *Die Täufer. Von der radikalen Reformation zu den Baptisten*, München.
Kaufmann, Thomas (2022): *Die Druckmacher: Wie die Generation Luther die erste Medienrevolution entfesselte*. München: C. H. Beck.
Kaufmann, Thomas (2024): *Der Bauernkrieg. Ein Medienereignis*, Freiburg/Basel/Wien.
Klein, Thomas (1975): 'Die Folgen des Bauernkriegs von 1525: Thesen und Antithesen zu einem vernachlässigten Thema', *Hessisches Jahrbuch für Landesgeschichte* 25, 65-116.
Kim, Min Hwan (2025): *Luther's View of Purgatory: An Examination of His Theological Understanding of Suffering as the Cross*, Eugene, Oregon.
Köhler, Hans-Joachim (1996): *Bibliographie der Flugschriften des 16. Jahrhunderts. Teil 1: Das frühe 16. Jahrhundert (1501–1530)*, vol. 3. Tübingen: Bibliotheca Academica.
Krümpelmann, Maximilian: 'The History of the Taylorian Copies', in Jones / Lähnemann (2020), xxxix–lxvi. Open access.
Lähnemann, Henrike and Eva Schlotheuber (2024): *The Life of Nuns. Love, Politics, and Religion in Medieval German Convents* , Cambridge (UK).
Lähnemann, Henrike (2016): 'Der Medinger 'Nonnenkrieg' aus der Perspektive der Klosterreform: Geistliche Selbstbehauptung 1479–1554', in *1517-1545: The Northern Experience. Mysticism, Art and Devotion between Late Medieval and Early Modern*, ed. Kees Scheepers et al., *Ons Geestelijk Erf* 87, 91–116.
Laube, Adolf and Hans Werner Seiffert (ed.) (1975): *Flugschriften der Bauernkriegszeit*, Berlin.
Marc'hadour, Germain (2010): 'Review of Erasmus' Defence of his *De libero arbitrio*', *Moreana* 47 (181–182), 293–302.
Markert, Gerhard (2008): *Menschen um Luther. Eine Geschichte der Reformation in Lebensbildern*, Ostfildern.
Martin Luther. Dokumente seines Lebens und Wirkens (1983), Weimar.

Micklich, Rahel (2025): *Spekulative Pädagogik. Johannes de Garlandia auf den Spuren des Alanus ab Insulis*, Brüssel.

Müller, Thomas T. (2021): Mörder ohne Opfer: Die Reichsstadt Mühlhausen und der Bauernkrieg in Thüringen, Petersberg.

Nüssel, Friederike (2000): *Allein aus Glauben. Zur Entwicklung der Rechtfertigungslehre in der konkordistischen und frühen nachkonkordistischen Theologie*, Göttingen.

Oldham, J. Basil (1958): *Blind Panels of English Binders*, Cambridge (UK).

Ostermann, Christina and Henrike Lähnemann (forthcoming), 'Friedrich Max Müller and the Acquisition of Reformation Pamphlets at the Taylor Institution Library', in: *Migration Collections: Translocation Research in Libraries and Archives, 1850–2025*. Special Issue of the *Forum for Modern Language Studies*, ed. Sophia Buck and Stefanie Hundehege.

Roper, Lyndal (2017): Martin Luther: Renegade and Prophet, London.

Roper, Lyndal (2025): Summer of Fire and Blood. The German Peasants' War, New York.

Schilling, Heinz (2017): *Martin Luther: Rebel in an Age of Upheaval*, trans. Rona Johnston, Oxford.

Scheck, Thomas P. (2013): 'John Fisher's Response to Martin Luther', in: *Franciscan Studies*, Vol. 71, 463–509.

Schwarz, Reinhard (1989): 'Thomas Müntzer und die Mystik', in: *Der Theologe Thomas Müntzer. Untersuchungen zu seiner Entwicklung und Lehre;* ed. by Siegfried Bräuer and Helmar Junghans, Berlin, 283–301.

Schwerhoff, Gerd (2024): *Der Bauernkrieg. Geschichte einer wilden Handlung*, München.

Sea, Thomas F. (1999): 'The Swabian League and Peasant Disobedience before the German Peasants' War of 1525', *The Sixteenth Century Journal* 30/1 (Spring, 1999), 89-111.

Steinmetz, Max (1971), *Das Müntzerbild von Martin Luther bis Friedrich Engels*, Berlin.

Streller, Siegfried (1970), *Hutten. Müntzer. Luther. Werke in zwei Bänden*, Berlin/Weimar.

The German Peasants' War: A History in Documents (1991), ed. Tom Scott and Robert W. Scribner, Amherst.

Vogler, Günter (^{3}1983): *Die Gewalt soll gegeben werden dem gemeinen Volk. Der deutsche Bauernkrieg 1525*, Berlin.

Wald, Berthold (2015): *Luthers Theologie und Anthropologie im Spiegel seiner Biographie*, Aachen.

Zöllner, Walter (1961), *Zur Geschichte des Großen Deutschen Bauernkrieges: Dokumente und Materialien*, Berlin.

Zschäbitz, Gerhard (1967), *Martin Luther – Größe und Grenze. 1. Teil 1483-1526*, Berlin.

Wolgast, Eike (1989): 'Die Obrigkeits- und Widerstandslehre Thomas Müntzers'; in: *Der Theologe Thomas Müntzer. Untersuchungen zu seiner Entwicklung und Lehre;* ed. by Siegfried Bräuer and Helmar Junghans, Berlin, 195–220.

3. Taylor Editions: Reformation Pamphlets

Open Access https://editions.mml.ox.ac.uk/publications/

1) Jones, Howard (ed.) (2017): *Martin Luther: Sendbrief vom Dolmetschen. An Open Letter on Translation.* Open Access.
2) Jones, Howard, Martin Keßler, Henrike Lähnemann and Christina Ostermann (eds.) (2018*): Martin Luther: Sermon von Ablass und Gnade, 95 Thesen. Sermon on Indulgences and Grace and the 95 Theses.* Open Access.
3) Jones, Howard and Henrike Lähnemann (eds.) (2020): *Martin Luther: Von der Freiheit eines Christenmenschen. On Christian Freedom.* Open Access.
4) Wareham, Edmund, Ulrich Bubenheimer and Henrike Lähnemann (eds.) (2021): *Martin Luther: Passional Christi und Antichristi. Passional of Christ and Antichrist.* Open Access.
5) Jones, Howard and Henrike Lähnemann (eds.) (2022): *Martin Luther: Ein Sendbrief vom Dolmetschen und Fürbitte der Heiligen. An Open Letter on Translation and the Intercession of Saints.* 2nd ed. Open Access.
6) Gieseler, Florian, Henrike Lähnemann and Timothy Powell (eds.) (2023): *Martin Luther: 'Mönchkalb' and 'Ursache und Antwort' Two Anti-Monastic Pamphlets from 1523.* Open Access here and here.
7) Flacke, Philip, Henrike Lähnemann, Jacob Ridley and Thomas Wood (eds.) (2024): Hans Sachs, Canon and Cobbler. A Reformation Dialogue in German, Dutch, and English. Open Access

Edition, Translation, Commentary
Wider die Rotten der Bauern
Against the Bands of Peasants

The edition is a semi-diplomatic transcription of the Nuremberg edition of the pamphlet in the Taylor Institution Library. Abbreviations have been resolved and marked in *italics*. r- and s-forms have been standardized, but not u/v- or i/j-forms. The original punctuation has been kept but the text has been divided into paragraphs.

The commentary consists of two sets of footnotes. Those on the edition side (left-hand pages) are not a full linguistic analysis, but are designed to help readers understand Luther's German and typographical features, comparing Early New High German (ENHG) forms with New High German (NHG), i.e. modern usage and English parallels, giving biblical references in the form of Martin Luther's own Bible translation (L45), the King James Version (KJV) and, for Old Testament references, the Vulgate in the late medieval form of the Clementine (VLC) since Luther had not fully finished his translation in 1525. The footnotes to the English translation (right-hand side) include historical background information.

The transcription was done by participants of the Sommerakademie der Studienstiftung in Oxford September 2025 and Rahel Micklich; the translation and linguistic footnotes are by Howard Jones and Henrike Lähnemann; historical footnotes were provided by Ryan Hampton and Henrike Lähnemann.
Online https://editions.mml.ox.ac.uk/editions/peasants-nuremberg/

(A1r) Wider die mordischen vnd reubischen Rotten der Pawren
Martinus Luther. Wittemberg.

Psalm .vij. Seine tück werden jn selbs treffen / Vnnd sein mutwill wirdt über jn außgehen.[1]

(A1v) Wider die stürmenden Pawren[2] / Martinus Luther

---

[1] Psalm 7 is presented in its title as a prayer by David for God's protection against his enemy. The German translation on the titlepage is closer to the Vulgate version than to the translation Luther eventually used for Psalm 7 in his German Bible. *Convertetur dolor ejus in caput ejus, et in verticem ipsius iniquitas ejus descendet.* (Vulgata Clementina [VLC] Ps 7:17). *His mischief shall return upon his own head, and his violent dealing shall come down upon his own pate.* (King James Version [KJV] Ps 7:16) *Sein vnglück wird auff seinen Kopff komen / Vnd sein freuel auff seine Scheittel fallen.* (Luther Bible of 1545 [L45] Ps 7:17). In the following, Bible references are given with a link to biblija.net which allows the parallel display of VLC, KJV, and L45.

[2] = NHG 'Bauern'. The use of p for initial b is typical of Franconian, the dialect of the Nuremberg area.

(A1r) Against the murdering and robbing bands of peasants,[3] by Martin Luther, Wittenberg[4]

Psalm 7: Their scheming will recoil on them, and their wilful arrogance will descend upon them.

(A1v) Against the rioting peasants. Martin Luther

---

[3] The Erfurt edition has *Wider die sturmenden Bawren Auch wider die reubischen vnd mŏrdisschen rotten der andern Bawren* (Against the rioting peasants. Also against the robbing and murdering bands of peasants). On the history behind the different versions of the title cf. chapter 1.1. and the list of different editions in chapter 3.2.

[4] The mention of Wittenberg on the titlepage could simply refer to the place where Martin Luther was writing, but also serves as authorisation, particularly since the actual printer, Friedrich Peypus in Nuremberg, does not appear on the titlepage.

(A2r) Im vorigen büchlin thurste⁵ ich die Pawren nicht vrteilen / weyl sie sich zu recht vn*d* besser unterricht erboten⁶ / Wie den*n* Christus gepeut / man soll nicht vrteylen / Matth[ei] .vij.⁷ Aber ehe den*n* ich mich vmbsihe / faren sie fort / vn*d* greyffen mit der faust drein / mit vergessen jrs erbietens / rauben vn*d* toben / vn*d* thun wie die rasenden hunde. Dabey man nu*n* wol sihet / was sie in jrem falschen sinn gehabt haben / vn*d* das eytel⁸ erlogen ding sey gewesen / was sie unter dem namen des Euangeli in den zwölff Artickeln haben fürgewendet. Kurtz vmb / eyttel Teuffels werck treyben sie / vnnd in sonderheyt / ists der Erzteuffel / der zu Mülhusen regiert / vnd nichts denn⁹ raub / mord / blutuergiessen anricht / wie dann Christus Johan[nis] .viij.¹⁰ von jm sagt / das er sey ein mörder von anbegynn / Nun den*n* sich solche Pawren vnd ellende leutte verfüren lassen / vn*d* anders thun / den*n* sie geredt haben / muß ich auch anders vo*n* jnen schreiben / vnd erstlich jre sunde für jre augen stellen / wie Gott Esaia¹¹ vn*d* Ezechiel¹² befelht / ob sich etlich erken*n*en wollten / Vn*d* darnach der welltliche*n* Oberkeyt gewissen / wie sie sich hyrin*n*en hallten solle*n* / vntertichten¹³

---

⁵ Past tense of 'turren' = dare, a MHG modal verb which becomes obsolete in the 16th century, FWb s.v. 'turren'.
⁶ Past tense from 'erbieten', to offer to do sth.; see two lines below.
⁷ Matthew 7:1 *RJchtet nicht / Auff das jr nicht gerichtet werdet.* (L45)
⁸ ENHG 'eitel' = completely, nothing but.
⁹ 'ENHG 'nichts denn' = 'nichts als' in NHG - this usage of 'mehr' only survives in the set expression 'mehr denn je'.
¹⁰ John 8:44 The passage characterises the devil as a murderer and spiritual father of liars, stating that his followers carry out his desires.
¹¹ Isaiah 58:1 *RVffe getrost / schone nicht / Erhebe deine stim wie eine Posaune / vnd verkündige meinem Volck jr vbertretten / vnd dem hause Jacob jre sunde.* (L45)
¹² Ezekiel 2:7 *Sondern du solt jnen mein wort sagen / sie gehorchen oder lassens / Denn es ist ein vngehorsam Volck.* (L45)
¹³ Probably a typographical error for 'unterrichten' (to instruct) which is used in edition A, but 'untertichten' can also be understood as a neologism for 'to tell in written form' (ENHG tichten = NHG 'dichten'). This relates to the 'gewissen' (conscience) of the 'Oberkeyt' (= NHG 'Obrigkeit', authority).

(A2r) In the previous pamphlet[14] I did not venture to judge the peasants, as they had offered to submit to the law and to instruction for their betterment, just as Christ commands us not to judge (Matthew 7). But before I even have time to look round,[15] off they go, taking matters violently into their own hands, forgetting their offer, thieving, and running riot like mad dogs.[16] From this we can now clearly see the deception they intended and that what they proposed in the *Twelve Articles*[17] in the name of the Gospel was nothing but lies. In short, they are just doing the work of the devil, and above all that archdevil who presides at Mühlhausen[18] and does nothing but stir up robbery, murder, and bloodshed – as Christ says of him in John 8, he has been a murderer from the beginning. Now since these peasants and wretches have allowed themselves to be led astray and are behaving differently than they promised to, I must write differently about them too and, first of all, set their sins before their eyes, as God commands Isaiah and Ezekiel to do, on the off-chance that some of them might see themselves for what they are; and then I must instruct the consciences of to the worldly authorities on how they should conduct themselves in this situation.

---

[14] The *Ermahnung zum Frieden* of 19 April 1525 (cf. chapter 3.1.) in fact "unequivocally condemned" the peasants, Roper (2017), 249.

[15] When Luther began writing these words on 6 May 1525, he had just returned from a lengthy ecclesiastical inspection tour where his audience was unsympathetic to his message of obedience to the authorities. This reception may have contributed to the tone of this pamphlet, cf. chapter 1.1; Schilling (2017), 250-59.

[16] In reality, the rebels limited violence almost exclusively to pillaging and destroying ecclesiastical institutions and castles to gather provisions and attract new followers. One exception was the so-called Weinsberg Massacre, which occurred near Heilbronn on Easter Sunday, on 16 April 1525, sparking outrage among the Empire's nobility. Lordly violence, on the other hand, was frequently personal, indiscriminate, and sadistic; Appold (2025), 58-107; Schwerhoff (2024), 217-24, 555-58.

[17] Luther's views on the *Twelve Articles* departed from that of his own patron, Elector Frederick the Wise, cf. chapter 1.1; Roper (2025), 270.

[18] Thomas Müntzer, the radical reformer of Mühlhausen, was known for his violent rhetoric, yet his movement was strikingly bloodless, cf. chapter 1.2; Müller (2021).

Dreyerley[19] grewliche sunden wider Gott vnd menschen laden dise Pawren auff sich / daran sie den tod verdienet haben an leybe vnnd seele manigfeltiglich.

Zum Ersten / das sie jrer Oberkeit trew vnd hulde geschworen haben / vnterthenig vnd gehorsam zuseyn / wie solchs Gott gepeut / da er spricht / Gebt dem Keiser was des Keisers ist[20] / Vnd Roma[nos] .xiij. Yderman sey der Oberkeyt vnterthan / etce.[21] Weyl sie aber disen gehorsam brechen mutwilliglich vnd mit freuel / vnnd darzu sich wider jre herren setzen / haben sie damit verwirckt leyb vnd seel / als die trewlose / meineydige / lugenhafftigen / vngehorsamen[22] buben vnd bößewicht pflegen zuthun / darumb auch. S. Paulus Roma[nos] .xiij. ein solch vrteil über sie fellet / Welche der gewalt (a2r) widerstreben die werdenn ein gericht über sich überkomen.[23] Welcher spruch auch die Pawren entlich treffen wirdt. es geschehe kurtz oder lange / denn Gott will trew vnd pflicht gehallten haben.

---

[19] Luther favoured lists which allowed him to order his arguments as in an academic debate, as he had done in the '95 Theses' but also in vernacular works such as the *Sermon von Ablass und Gnade*. He is not always consistent in seeing these lists through to the end.

[20] Luke 20:25 *And he said unto them, Render therefore unto Caesar the things which be Caesar's, and unto God the things which be God's* (KJV). *Er aber sprach zu jnen / So gebet dem Keiser / was des Keisers ist / vnd Gotte / was Gottes ist* (L45).

[21] Romans 13:1 *Let every soul be subject unto the higher powers. For there is no power but of God: the powers that be are ordained of God* (KJV). *JEderman sey vnterthan der Oberkeit / die gewalt vber jn hat. Denn es ist keine Oberkeit / on von Gott / Wo aber Oberkeit ist / die ist von Gott verordnet* (L45).

[22] Mix of strong (*trewlose* and *meineydige*) and weak (*lugenhafftigen* and *vngehorsamenn*) adjective endings.

[23] Romans 13:2 *Whosoever therefore resisteth the power, resisteth the ordinance of God: and they that resist shall receive to themselves damnation* (KJV). *Wer sich nu wider die Oberkeit setzet / Der widerstrebet Gottes ordnung / Die aber widerstreben / werden vber sich ein Vrteil empfahen* (L45).

These peasants are burdening themselves with three appalling sins against God and mankind, and for these they now deserve death many times over in body and soul. First, they have sworn to be true and loyal to those with authority over them,[24] to be subservient and obedient, as God commands when he says: 'Give to Caesar the things that are Caesar's', and in Romans 13: 'Let everybody be subject to authority', etc.[25] But now that they are deliberately and wickedly breaking this vow of obedience and, what is more, setting themselves against their masters, they have thereby forfeited body and soul, as is the way with faithless, perjured, lying, disobedient scoundrels and villains.[26] Which is also why Saint Paul passes this judgement on them, saying in Romans 13: 'Those who resist authority (a2r) will bring judgement upon themselves.' These words will eventually, sooner or later, hit their mark with the peasants as well, because God wants loyalty and duty to be observed.

---

[24] Luther refers here to the *Huldigung*, the collective oath which a community (*Gemeinde*) swore to its feudal lord. By the early sixteenth century, the *Huldigung* was being weaponised in legal practice to undermine peasants' right to assemble and to seek legal redress against their lords. Communal assembly and reciprocal oath-taking, acts which were central to any community's decision to make a legal appeal, were increasingly held to violate the *Huldigung* and branded as "treasonous" (*meineidig*), cf. Sea (1999), 95.

[25] Article 3 of the *Twelve Articles* references this same verse: "Not that we wish to be completely free and to have no authority, for God does not teach us that... we will gladly obey our elected and appointed rulers (whom God has ordained over us) in all reasonable and Christian matters. We have no doubt that, as true and genuine Christians, you will gladly release us from serfdom, or else show us from the Gospel that we are serfs"., cf. *The German Peasants' War* (1991), no. 125, 202.

[26] Such language was part of a vocabulary used to defame peasant resistance as wilful, dangerous, and seditious. Another early example was the subdual of the Poor Conrad movement in Württemberg. The imperial ban of 19 September 1514 labelled their actions as "having served malicious, evil, dangerous, and harmful conspiracy unjust disobedience, shame, and disgrace, shedding blood and killing in an impetuous, tyrannical manner". (*der boshafftigen übeln geverlichen und schedlichen Conspiration... zů unbillicher ungehorsam schmach und verachtung... ungestümben tyrannischen blůt vergiessen und todschlegen... gedient haben*), cf. Blickle (1986), S88-S97; for the ban placed on the Poor Conrad, see Haupstaatsarchiv Stuttgart A 45 Bü 11 Um. 5 Nr. 1.

Zum Andern / das sie Auffrur anrichten / rauben vnd plundern mit freuel Clöster vnnd Schlösser / die nicht jr seind damit sie als die offenlichen strassenreuber vnd mörder / alleine wol zwiffeltig den tod an leyb vnnd seele verschulden. Auch ein auffrürischer mensch / den man des bezeugen kan / schon in Gottes vnnd Keyserlicher Acht[27] ist / das / wer am ersten kan vnnd mag denselben erwürgen / recht vnd wol thut. Denn über einen offenlichen auffrürgen / ist ein iglicher mensch / beyde oberrichter vnd scharffrichter / gleych als wenn ein fewr angehet / wer am ersten kan lesschen / der ist der beste / denn Auffrur ist nicht ein schlechter[28] mord / sondern wie ein gros fewr das ein land anzündet vnd verwustet / also bringt Auffrur mit sich ein land vol mords / blutuergissen / vnnd macht widwyn vnd waisen / vnd verstöret alles / wie das allergrössest unglück Drumb soll hie zuschmeissen[29] / wurgen vnd stechen / heymlich[30] / oder offenlich / wer da kan / vnd gedencke / das nicht gifftigers / schedlichers / teuffelischers seyn kan / denn ein auffrürischer mensch / gleich als wenn man einen tollen hund totschlahen muß / schlegstu nit / so schlegt er dich vnd ein gantz land mit dir /

---

[27] in der Acht sein = to be banned, cf. FWb <u>acht2, sense 2</u>. The 'Reichsacht' (imperial ban), declared by the Holy Roman Emperor (hence 'Keyserliche Acht' here) or the Imperial Diet or by courts meant that people under this ban lost all their rights and possessions. They were legally considered dead, and anyone was allowed to rob or kill them without legal consequences. The 'Acht' automatically followed the excommunication of a person, extending also to anyone offering help to a person under the ban. Luther argues that the rebellious peasants have been put automatically under the ban and are therefore no longer protected by law.
[28] = NHG 'schlicht'.
[29] = NHG 'zerschmeißen'.
[30] The line from *Drumb* to *heymlich* is underlined by a contemporary reader with the comment *gemachh* ('take it easy!') in the right-hand margin, cf. chapters 1.1 and 3.2.

Secondly, they are starting a rebellion and brazenly robbing and looting monasteries[31] and castles that are not theirs and so, as highwaymen and murderers, they fully deserve death in body and soul twice over just for this. Moreover, anyone who is demonstrably rebellious is already an outlaw before God and the emperor, so the first person able and willing to put them to death is well within their rights to do so. For if someone is openly stirring rebellion, everyone is both their judge and executioner, just as, when a fire breaks out, the first person who can put it out is the best person to do so. For rebellion is not mere murder, but it is like a great fire that sets ablaze and lays waste a whole land; likewise, rebellion brings murder and bloodshed to the whole land and makes widows and orphans and destroys everything, like the very worst disaster. So, in this situation, whoever can do so should smash, throttle, and stab them, in secret or in the open, and should remember that there can be nothing more poisonous, destructive, devilish than a rebellious person; just as, when you have to put to death a mad dog, if you do not slay it, it slays you and takes a whole land with you.[32]

---

[31] The working group "Visualising the Destruction of Convents & Monasteries during the German Peasants' War" has recently identified 623 monasteries and convents which were affected by the conflict, whether through damage, destruction, plunder, threats, or being forced to make an inventory of their goods. There were an estimated 1,200 ecclesiastical institutions in the area touched by the war, meaning that more than 50% were affected. See Louisa Bergold, Charlotte Gauthier, Lyndal Roper, Edmund Wareham Wanitzek, https://germanpeasantswar.web.ox.ac.uk/.

[32] Luther echoed a contemporary discourse which characterised the consequences of peasant resistance in apocalyptic terms, cf. *Der Bundschuh* (1927), no. 21, 110–11.

Zum Dritten / das sie solche schreckliche / grewlicke sůnde / mit dem Euangelio decken / nennen sich Christliche brůder / nemen eyd vnd hulde³³ / vnd zwingen die leutte / zu solchen greweln / mit jnen zuhallten / damit sie die allergrösten Gottslesterer vnd schender seines heyligen namens werden / vnd ehren vnd dienen also dem Teuffel / vnter dem scheyn des Euangelij / daran sie wol zehen mal den tod verdienen an leyb vnd seele / das ich heßlicher sunde nie gehört habe. Vnd achte³⁴ auch / das der Teuffel den iůngsten tag fůle / das³⁵ er solch vnerhörte stůck fůrnimpt / als solt er sagenn / Es ist das letzte / drumb solt es das (a2v) ergste seyn / vnd will die grundsuppen³⁶ růren / vnd den poden gar außstossen³⁷ / Gott wöll jm weren³⁸. Da sihe / welch ein mechtiger Fůrst der Teuffel ist / wie er die wellt in henden hat / vnd ineinander mengen kan / der so pald so vil tausent Pawren / fangen / verfůren / verblenden / verstocken / vnd empören³⁹ kan / vnd mit jn machen was sein aller wůtigister grym fůrnimpt.

---

³³ 'Hulde nehmen' = 'sich huldigen lassen', to take oaths of loyalty, cf. DWb s.v. huld.
³⁴ In ENHG, the personal pronoun is sometimes missing, here 'ich'; ENHG 'achte' = NHG 'erachte', in the sense of 'reckon, guess, consider, think'.
³⁵ = NHG 'so dass'.
³⁶ FWb s.v. 'grundsuppe' = unusable dregs of a barrel, mob.
³⁷ FWb s.v. 'ausstossen' 4 (phrase 'dem fas den boden ausstossen' = 'to bring something to a violent end').
³⁸ Optative construction = NHG 'Gott möge ihm das verwehren'.
³⁹ FWb s.v. 'empören' 4 = to provoke to rebellion.

Thirdly, they use the Gospel[40] as a cover for these horrific, abominable sins, call themselves Christian brethren,[41] swear oaths and take vows of loyalty,[42] and force the people to go along with them in these abominations. In doing this they become the greatest ever blasphemers of God and slanderers of his holy name and so honour and serve the devil under the pretence of the Gospel, which means they deserve death in body and soul a good ten times over; I have never heard of a sin more heinous. I also think the devil can sense Judgement Day coming, carrying out such unheard-of atrocities, as if to say, "This is the last one, so it had better be the (a2v) worst", and he wants to scrape the barrel and even smash the bottom out of it completely – may God prevent him! Just look what a powerful ruler the devil is, how he holds the world in his hands and can throw it into confusion, able as he is to take in so many thousands of peasants so quickly, lead them astray, blind them, harden them, and stir them into rebellion, and do with them whatever his deranged fury prompts him to.

---

[40] The Holy Gospel (*das Heilige Evangelium*) was one of several watchwords of the Peasants' War movement. The first of the *Twelve Articles* stipulated that each community should have the right to choose its own preacher, who should "preach the holy Gospel to us purely and clearly, without any human additions to doctrines and commandments". Luther rejected the rebels' understanding of the Gospel as a conflation of temporal and spiritual matters, cf. Schwerhoff (2024), 535-40; for the *Twelve Articles*, cf. Scott and Scribner (1991), no. 125, 200-204.

[41] For the importance of "brotherhood" as another unifying watchword of the movement, see chapter 1.1 and Roper (2025), 279-318.

[42] Such oaths were a constituent part of rebel organisation, a bonding experience which fostered links of brotherhood and mutual support. A kind of inversion or "flattening" of the hierarchical oath of feudal loyalty sworn to lords, they were increasingly criminalised from the late Middle Ages, and especially from the 1490s in response to the Bundschuh movement, cf. Roper (2025), 138-39; Sea (1999), 95.

Es hillft⁴³ auch die Pawren nicht / das sie fůrgeben / Gen[esis] .j. vnd .ij.⁴⁴ Es seyen alle ding frey vnd gemeyne⁴⁵ geschaffen / vnd das wir alle gleych getaufft seind. Den*n* im newen Testame*n*t hellt vnd gillt⁴⁶ Moses nicht / sondern da stehet vnser meister Christus / vn*d* wirfft⁴⁷ vns mit leyb vn*d* gut vnter den Keiser vn*d* welltlich recht / da er spricht / Gebt dem Keiser was das Keisers ist.⁴⁸ So spricht auch Paulus Roma[nos] .xij. zu allen getaufften Christen / Yderman sey der gewallt vnterthan.⁴⁹ Vnd Petrus / Seyt vnterthan aller menschlicher ordnu*n*g.⁵⁰ Diser lere Christi seind wir schuldig zugeleben / wie der vatter vom hymel gebeut vnnd sagt / Dis ist mein lieber Sůn / den hŏret.⁵¹

---

⁴³ 'helfen' can be constructed with accusative instead of dative in ENHG.
⁴⁴ Genesis chapter 1 and 2: creation of the world.
⁴⁵ FWb s.v. 'gemein' 6 = NHG 'allgemein': common, universal, shared.
⁴⁶ = NHG 'hält und gilt', legal formula for something that will last and be legally binding.
⁴⁷ 'unterwerfen' can be used as a separable verb in ENHG, retaining here more of the violent literal sense of 'to throw under', a loan translation from Latin 'subjicere'.
⁴⁸ Lk 20:25: *And he said unto them, Render therefore unto Caesar the things which be Caesar's, and unto God the things which be God's* (KJV). *Er aber sprach zu jnen / So gebet dem Keiser / was des Keisers ist / vnd Gotte / was Gottes ist* (L45).
⁴⁹ Actually Romans 13:1: *Let every soul be subject unto the higher powers. For there is no power but of God: the powers that be are ordained of God* (KJV). *JEderman sey vnterthan der Oberkeit / die gewalt vber jn hat. Denn es ist keine Oberkeit / on von Gott / Wo aber Oberkeit ist / die ist von Gott verordnet* (L45).
⁵⁰ 1 Peter 2:13: *Submit yourselves to every ordinance of man for the Lord's sake: whether it be to the king, as supreme* (KJV). *SEid vnterthan aller menschlicher Ordnung / vmb des HErrn willen / Es sey dem Könige als dem Obersten* / (L45).
⁵¹ Matthew 17:5: *While he yet spake, behold, a bright cloud overshadowed them: and behold a voice out of the cloud, which said, This is my beloved Son, in whom I am well pleased; hear ye him* (KJV). *Da er noch also redete / sihe / da vberschattet sie eine liechte Wolcken. Vnd sihe / eine stimme aus der wolcken sprach / Dis ist mein lieber Son / an welchem ich wolgefallen habe / Den solt jr hören* (L45).

Nor does it help the peasants when they claim that, according to Genesis chapters 1 and 2, all things are created free and common to all,[52] and that we all baptized alike. For in the New Testament Moses is not a binding authority, but there our Master Christ stands and casts us, in person and property, under the emperor and secular law, when he says: "Give to Caesar what is Caesar's". Likewise, Paul says in his letter to the Romans, chapter 12 [sic!], to all baptized Christians: "Everyone must be subject to those in power', and Peter says: "Be subject to all human authority". We are obliged to live according to this teaching of Christ, as the Father commands from heaven, saying: "This is my beloved Son, listen to him".

---

[52] Luther is exaggerating in characterising the rebels' demands for the abolition of the "small tithe" *(Kleinzehnt)* on livestock (Article 2 of the *Twelve Articles*) and free access to ponds (Article 4), woods (Article 5), fields, and meadows (Article 10) as a claim that "all things" were free; cf. Scott and Scribner (1991), No. 125, 200-204.

Denn die tauffe macht nicht leyb vnd gut frey / sondern die seelen. Auch macht das Euangelion nicht die güter gemeyn / on[53] alleine welche solchs williglich von jn selbs thun wöllen / wie die Aposteln vnd jünger / Act[a] .iiij. thetten / welche nicht die frembden güter Pilati vnd Herodis gemeyn zuseyn fodderten / wie vnser vnsinnige Paurn toben / sonder jr eygen güter.[54] Aber vnser Pawren wöllen der andern frembden güter gemein haben / vnd jr eygen für sich behallten. Das seind mir feine Christen / Ich meyn das kein Teuffel mehr in der helle sey / sonder allzumal in die Pawren seind gefaren. Es ist überauß vnd über alle masse das wüten.[55]

---

[53] = NHG 'ohne' in the sense of 'außer'.
[54] Acts 4:32–35: *And the multitude of them that believed were of one heart and of one soul: neither said any of them that ought of the things which he possessed was his own; but they had all things common. …* (KJV). *DEr menge aber der Gleubigen war ein Hertz vnd eine Seele. Auch keiner sagete von seinen Gütern / das sie sein weren / sondern es war jnen alles gemein…* (L45).
[55] Last sentence from *Ich meyn* to *wüten* underlined.

For baptism does not make person and property free, but the soul. Nor does the Gospel make goods common to all, except only in the case of those who voluntarily, of their own accord, do as the apostles and disciples did (Acts 4), when they demanded not that the goods of Pilate and Herod, which did not belong to them, be common to all, as our demented peasants do in their ranting and raving, but their own goods. Our peasants, on the other hand, want the goods of others, which do not belong to them, to be common to all, and to keep their own for themselves. To me they are fine Christians! I don't think there is a single devil left in hell: they have all gone into the peasants.[56] This madness has gone too far, beyond all bounds.

---

[56] Luther's belief in demonic possession in some ways was similar to peasant religiosity and its belief in spirits and the efficacy of exorcism rituals. *Wider die Rotten* in particular shows Luther "operating with an archaic belief system that has much more in common with that of the peasants themselves than with his humanistically inclined colleagues", Appold (2025), 179. Such allusions might therefore possibly be read literally and Luther's belief that the devil was behind the peasants' actions could be one of the reasons for the intemperance of his language.

16   *Edition 'Wider die Rotten' (Nuremberg)*

Weyl den*n* nun die Pawren auff sich laden / beyde Gott vn*d* menschen / vn*d* so manigfelltiglich schon des tods an leyb und seel schuldig seind / vnd keins rechten gestehen⁵⁷ noch warten / sondern ymer fort toben / muß ich hie die welltliche Oberkeyt vnterrichten wie sie hierin*n*e mit gutem gewissen faren solle*n*. Erstlich der Oberkeyt / so⁵⁸ da kan vn*d* will / on vorgehend erbie(a3r)ten zum recht vn*d* billigkeyt / solche Pawren schlahen vn*d* straffen / will ich nicht wehren / ob sie⁵⁹ gleych das Euangelion nit leydet / Den*n* sie hat des⁶⁰ gut recht / Sintemal⁶¹ die Pawren nun nicht mehr vmb das Euangelion fechten / sonder seind offenlich worde*n* trewlose / meyneydige / vngehorsame / auffrürische / mörder / reuber / gottslesterer / welche auch Heydenische Oberkeyt zustraffen recht vn*d* macht hat / ia dazu schuldig ist / solche Buben zustraffen. Denn darumb tregt sie das schwert / vnd ist Gottes dienerin über den so übelst thut / Roma[nos] .xiij.⁶²

---

⁵⁷ FWb s.v. 'gestehen' ij 'recht gestehen' = vor Gericht erscheinen.
⁵⁸ In ENHG, 'so' can be used instead of relative pronouns.
⁵⁹ This either refers back to 'Oberkeyt' or is an elliptic construction referring to 'die Gewalt' or similar: 'even if it [i.e. exercising brutal power] is not permitted by the Gospel'.
⁶⁰ 'des' = NHG 'dessen'; ENHG 'haben' constructed here with genitive: 'they have a good right of this', i.e. 'a perfect right to do this'.
⁶¹ Now obsolete, equivalent English 'since'.
⁶² 'Oberkeyt' (= NHG 'Obrigkeit') is here, as in Luther's Bible translation, treated as female personification due to the predominant gender of abstract nouns, Rom 13:3–4: *For rulers are not a terror to good works, but to the evil. Wilt thou then not be afraid of the power? do that which is good, and thou shalt have praise of the same: For he is the minister of God to thee for good. But if thou do that which is evil, be afraid; for he beareth not the sword in vain: for he is the minister of God, a revenger to execute wrath upon him that doeth evil* (KJV). *Denn die Gewaltigen sind nicht den guten wercken / Sondern den bösen zu fürchten. Wiltu dich aber nicht fürchten fur der Oberkeit / so thue gutes / so wirstu lob von derselbigen haben / Denn sie ist Gottes Dienerin / dir zu gut. Thustu aber böses / so fürchte dich / Denn sie tregt das Schwert nicht vmb sonst / Sie ist Gottes Dienerin / eine Racherin zur straffe vber den / der böses thut* (L45).

Since the peasants are now turning both God and the people against them and are thus already guilty of death in body and soul many times over, and they neither appear in court nor are prepared to do so,[63] but continue to run riot, I must here instruct the secular authorities how they should proceed with a clear conscience in this matter. First, I do not wish to oppose rulers who are willing and able to strike down and punish these peasants without submitting beforehand (a3r) to a proper legal process, even those rulers who do not accept the Gospel, for they are well within their rights to do so, since the peasants are now no longer fighting for the Gospel, but have publicly shown themselves to be faithless, perjured, disobedient, rebellious murderers, robbers, blasphemers, whom even heathen rulers have the right and authority to punish – indeed, they are obliged to punish such scoundrels. After all, that is why those in authority bear the sword and are God's handmaidens against the one who does evil (Romans 13).[64]

---

[63] Arbitration in court was a standard means of resolving disputes between lords and vassals in early 16th century society. However, the process was frequently lengthy and costly, especially for peasants who stood to lose much by leaving their farms to press legal claims in distant cities. Lords sometimes referred cases to distant (or partial) courts which were either too far for their subjects to reach or where the latter could not expect a fair hearing. This was allegedly a cause of the Bundschuh movement of 1513. Yet Luther certainly erred in attributing to the rebels an unwillingness to submit to arbitration, cf. Bierbrauer (1980), 1-68.

[64] Luther had already affirmed this in his 1523 pamphlet *Von weltlicher Obrigkeit: Wie weit man dem weltlichen Regiment gehorchen soll* (WA 11, 245-281) on how far obedience is owed to secular authority, specifically WA 11, 257, 17-19.

Aber die Oberkeyt so Christlich ist / vnd das Euangelion leydet[65] / derhalbenn auch die Pawren keinen scheyn[66] wider sie haben / soll hie mit forcht handeln. Vnnd zum ersten die sachen Gott heymgeben[67] / vnd bekennen / das wir solchs wol verdient haben. Dazu sorgen[68] / das Gott villeicht den Teuffel also errege zu gemeyner[69] straffe Teutschs lannds[70]. Darnach demůtiglich bitten wider den Teuffel umb hůlffe /[71] Denn wir fechten hie nicht alleine wider blut vnnd fleysch / sondern wider die geystlichen bösewicht in der lufft / welche mit gebett müssen angegriffen werden.[72] Wenn nun das hercze so gegen Gott gerichtet ist / das man seinen göttlichen willen leßt wallten / ob er vns wölle oder nicht wölle zu Fürsten vnd herren haben / soll man sich gegen die tollen Pawren zum überfluß (ob[73] sie es wol nicht werdt seind) zu recht vnd gleychem erbieten. Darnach wo das nicht helffen will / flucks[74] zum schwert greyffen.

---

[65] FWb s.v. '¹leiden' 4: to permit, allow.
[66] DWb s.v. 'schein' 8: technical expression for evidence in a court case.
[67] ENHG '(an)heim geben / stellen' = put back into the responsibility ('home') of somebody.
[68] FWb s.v. '(be)sorgen' 1 = NHG 'befürchten': to be apprehensive.
[69] FWb s.v. 'gemein' 6 = NHG 'allgemein': common, universal, shared.
[70] 'Deutsch landt' at that time is not yet the NHG compound 'Deutschland' with a clear definition but refers to the whole cluster of German-speaking lands within the Holy Roman Empire ('Heiliges Römisches Reich deutscher Nation').
[71] The whole construction from *Aber die Oberkeyt* at the start of the page up to here is syntactically one sentence, with fluid transitions between the parts of the argument; *so Christlich ... leydet* is an embedded relative clause on which *derhalbenn... wider sie haben* is dependent as a further subordinate clause.
[72] Eph 6:12: *For we wrestle not against flesh and blood, but against principalities, against powers, against the rulers of the darkness of this world, against spiritual wickedness in high places* (KJV). *Denn wir haben nicht mit Fleisch vnd Blut zu kempffen / Sondern mit Fürsten vnd Gewaltigen / nemlich / mit den Herrn der Welt / die in der finsternis dieser Welt herrschen / mit den bösen Geistern vnter dem Himel* (L45).
[73] ENHG 'obwohl' can be split, as here.
[74] DWb s.v. 'flugs': lexicalized term derived from the genitive of 'Flug' (flight) = in a hurry, directly.

But rulers who are Christian and accept the Gospel – meaning that the peasants do not even have admissible evidence against them – should in this case act in fear[75] and first entrust the matter to God and confess that we have fully deserved this; they should also be concerned that this is perhaps how God is stirring up the devil to inflict collective punishment on the German lands; and then they should humbly ask for help against the devil. For here we are fighting not just against flesh and blood, but against spiritual evil-doers up above[76] who must be attacked with prayer. Then, when our hearts are so directed towards God as to let his divine will be done, whether He wants us to be princes and lords or not, we should go beyond what is required and show ourselves open to justice and fairness towards those mad peasants (even though they are quite unworthy of it); finally, if that doesn't help, take up your swords straight away.

---

[75] Fear of God in the biblical sense of awe and reverence, rather than in a modern sense of alarm and terror.

[76] Luther is also referencing Ephesians 2:2 here which refers to the devil as 'the prince of the power of the air'.

Denn ein Fürst vnd Herr muß hie dencken wie er Gottes amptman[77] vnnd seins zorns diener[78] ist / Romano[s] .xiij.[79] dem das schwert über solche buben befolhen ist / Vnd sich eben so hoch für[80] Gott versündigt / wo er nicht strafft vnd wehret / und sein ampt nicht volfüret / als wenn einer mördet / dem das schwert nicht befolhen ist. Denn wo er kan vnd strafft nicht / es sey durch mord oder blutuergiessen / so ist er schuldig an allem mord vnd übel / das solche buben bege[h]en[81] / als der da mutwilliglich durch nachlassen seins göttlichen befelhs / zulesst solche boßheyt zu (a3v) üben / so ers wol wehren kan vnd schuldig ist. Darumb ist hie nicht zuschlaffen. Es gillt auch nicht hie gedult oder barmhertzigkeyt Es ist des schwerts vnd zorns zeyt hie vnd nicht der genaden zeyt.

---

[77] The position of the genitive is more flexible in ENHG, coming more often before the noun on which it is dependent, see also below at the end of the paragraph 'des schwerts vnd zorns zeyt' and 'der genaden zeyt'.

[78] The Lutheran concept of the 'Amtmann' is not so much referring to a specific position as steward but to somebody acting according to their office ('Amt') and estate as by divine ordination. The princes hold their office from God as his steward; see the definition in FWb s.v. 'amptman' 'dem in einer sozialen Ordnung eine bestimmte, meist administrative Funktion unterschiedlichen Ranges zugeteilt ist, Amtsperson, Träger, Inhaber eines Amtes'.

[79] Rom 13:3–4, as above.

[80] ENHG 'für' = NHG 'vor'.

[81] This edition has 'begeben' which is clearly a typo. The h-form in this font face has a rounded right stroke which makes it look similar to a b. The mistake is shared by the three editions printed in Nuremberg; all the other editions have 'begehen' which points to two printers using an edition issued by the third as their model, showing how the local circulation of Reformation material worked.

For a prince and lord must consider here that he is God's bailiff and the servant of his wrath (Romans 13),[82] to whom the sword is entrusted over such scoundrels, and that he sins before God just as much if he does not punish and defend and does not exercise his office, as if someone to whom the sword is not entrusted commits murder. For if he can punish and does not do so, even if by murder or bloodshed, he is guilty of all the murder and evil that these scoundrels commit, as by neglecting his divine command he wilfully allows them to practise such wickedness (a3v) when he is quite able and obliged to prevent it. Now is not the time for sleeping. Nor are patience and mercy in order here. Now is time for the sword and for wrath, and not the time for grace.

---

[82] Luther repeatedly used this verse to justify his calls for a harsh response to the uprisings – and not just in this pamphlet. In a letter of 4 or 5 May to Johann Rühel, councillor to Count Albrecht of Mansfeld, he urged Rühel not to counsel lenience against the rebels and cited Romans 13:4. See *WA* Br 3, no. 860, 480.

So soll nun die Oberkeyt hie getrost fort tringen / vnd mit gutem gewissen dreyn schlahen / weyl[83] sie eine ader[84] regen kan / denn hie ist das vortail[85] / das die Pawren böse gewissen vnnd vnrechte sachen haben / vnd welcher Pawr darüber erschlagen wirdt / mit leyb vnd seel verloren vnnd ewig des Teuffels ist. Aber die Oberkeyt hat ein gut gewissen vnnd rechte sachen / vnd kan zu Gott also sagen mit aller sicherheyt des hertzens / Sihe mein Gott / du hast mich zum Fürsten oder herren gesetzt daran ich nicht kan zweyffeln / vnd hast mir das schwert befolhen über die übelthetter / Rom[anos] .xiij.[86] Es ist dein wort vnd mag nicht liegen // So muß ich solch ampt / bey verlust deiner gnaden außrichten / So ists auch offentlich / das dise Pawren vilfaltig vor dir vnd vor der wellt den tod verdienet / vnd mir zu straffen befolhen. Willtu nun mich durch sie lassen tödten / vnd mir die Oberkeyt wider nemen vnd vntergehen lassen / wolan / so geschehe dein wille. So sterbe ich doch vnnd gehe vnter in deinem Göttlichen befelh vnd wort / vnd werd erfunden im gehorsam deines befelhs vnd meines ampts. Drumb will ich straffen vnd schlahen so lange ich eine ader regen[87] kan / du wirsts wol richten vnd machen.

---

[83] ENHG '(die)weil' = English 'while'.
[84] FWb. s.v. 'ader' 4: muscle; *die bauernadern erzeigen* = to show one's strength.
[85] 'Vorteil' in NHG is masculine but Luther consistently uses the older neuter form, DWb s.v. vorteil.
[86] Once again Romans 13:4, see above.
[87] Luther drives home his message to the princes by reformulating his advice to attack to the princes in the form of a prayer with the same verbs (*schlahen, ader regen*).

Those in authority, then, should now confidently press ahead and strike out with a clear conscience as long as they can move a muscle.[88] For in this case it is an advantage that the peasants have a bad conscience and an unjust cause, and that any peasant who is struck down over this is lost in body and soul and belongs to the devil forever. But rulers have a clear conscience and a just cause and can say to God with all certainty in their hearts: "Look, my God, you have appointed me as a prince or a lord – of this I can have no doubt – and you have entrusted me with the sword over evildoers (Romans 13). It is your word and it cannot lie, so I must carry out the duties of this office or forfeit your grace. It is also evident that these peasants have deserved death many times over, before you and before the world, and I am entrusted with their punishment. If you now wish to let me be killed by them and to have my authority taken away and destroyed, well then, let your will be done. But then I shall die and perish by your divine command and your word and I shall be seen to have obeyed your command and my office. I shall therefore punish and strike them as long as I can move a muscle. You will bring this about and make it right."[89]

---

[88] When Luther started writing on 6 May 1525, the 'striking out' was already well under way. The first pitched battle of the war was fought at Leipheim, near Ulm, on 4 April 1525. Many members of the public would read these words shortly after the uprisings had ended in slaughter in Böblingen, Frankenhausen, and Saverne on 12, 15, and 17 May, contributing to perceptions of the pamphlet as excessive, cf. chapter 1.1; Roper (2025), 269–71; Kaufmann (2024), 200–1.

[89] By reframing the lords' campaign as a crusade, Luther reflected a view held by many of the lords themselves, defining peasants as religious enemies and heretics, cf. Appold (2025), 103; Bischoff (2010), 181-183.

Also kans denn geschehen / das wer auff der Oberkeyt seyten erschlagen wirdt / ein rechter merterer vor Gott sey / so er mit solchem gewissen streyt / wie gesagt ist. Denn er gehet in Göttlichem wort vnnd gehorsam. Widerumb / was auff der Pawren seyten vmbkompt / ein ewiger hellebrandt ist / denn er füret das schwert wider Gottes wort vnd gehorsam / vnd ist ein Teuffels glied. Vnd obs gleych geschehe / das die Pawren oblegen / da Gott für sey / denn Gott seind alle ding müglich[90] / vnd wir nicht wissen / ob er villeicht zum vorlaufft des iüngsten (a4r) tags (welcher nicht ferne seyn will) wölle durch den Teuffel alle ordnung vnd oberkeyt zůstören / vnnd die wellt in einen wůsten hauffen werffen / So sterben doch sicher / vnnd gehen zuscheyttern mit gutem gewissen / die in jrem schwertampt funden werden / vnd lassen dem Teuffel das welltlich reich / vnd nemen dafür das ewige reich. Solch wunderliche zeyten seind itzt / das ein Fürst den hymel mit plutuergiessen verdienen kan / baß / denn andere mit betten.

---

[90] Cf. Jesus' words Mt 19:26: *Bey den Menschen ists vmmüglich / Aber bey Gott sind alle ding müglich* (L45) and Mk 10:27: *Bey den Menschen ists vmmüglich / Aber nicht bey Gott / Denn alle ding sind müglich bey Gott* (L45).

Thus it may be the case that anyone who is slain on the side of the authorities[91] is a true martyr before God, given that he is fighting with the kind of conscience just described, for he is acting obediently according to God's word. Conversely, anyone who perishes on the side of the peasants will burn in hell forever, for he wields the sword disobediently against God's word and is an instrument of the devil. And even if it should happen that the peasants are victorious, supposing God favours them – for all things are possible for God, and we do not know whether he perhaps wishes to destroy all order and authority through the devil as a prelude to the Last (a4r) Day,[92] which cannot be far off, and cast the world into a desolate heap – yet nevertheless those who are found to have exercised their authority with the sword will certainly die in peace and perish with a clear conscience, leaving the kingdom of the world to the devil and occupying the everlasting kingdom instead. These are strange times, when a prince can earn his place in heaven by shedding blood better than others can by praying.

---

[91] Very few were slain on the side of the authorities. While it is hard to assess figures for the entire war, many battles saw lordly casualties in the low double digits or fewer. In the battle of Leipheim, on 4 April 1525, for example, the armies of the Swabian League reportedly suffered no losses, while perhaps as many as 50 percent of the rebel army of 4,000 was killed. At Böblingen, on 12 May 1525, the League suffered losses of no more than 35 killed, while perhaps 6,000 rebels lost their lives. Estimates of aggregate losses on the rebel side have generally ranged between 70,000 and 100,000, cf. Schwerhoff (2024), 174-175 & 374; Franz (1933), 461; Klein (1975), 77.

[92] Luther expresses similar apocalyptic views in his interpretation of the monk-calf as a sign that the Last Judgement was near, cf. Gieseler & al. (2023), 3.

Am ende ist noch ein sache / die billich soll die Oberkeyt bewegen / Denn die Pawren lassen jn nicht benůgen / das sie des Teuffels seind / sondern zwingen vnd dringen vil frommer leute die es vngerne thun / zu jrem Teuffelischen bunde / vnd machen dieselbigen also teylhafftig aller jrer boßheyt vnd verdamnis. Denn wer mit jn[93] bewilliget[94] / der fert auch mit jn zum Teufel / vnd ist schuldig aller ůbelthat die sie begehen / vnd mův́ssens doch thun / weyl sie so schwachs glaubens seind / das sie nicht widerstehen. Denn hundert to᷎dte solt ein frommer Christ leyden / ehe er ein harbreit in der Pawren sache bewilliget. O vil merterer kundten itzt werden durch die plutdůrstigen Pawren vnd mordpropheten[95]. Nun solcher gefangener vnter den Pawren / sollten sich die Oberkeyt erbarmen / vnd wenn sie sonst keine sache hetten / das schwert getrȯst wider die Pawren gehen zulassen / vnd selbs leyb vnd gut dran zusetzen / so were doch dise ůberig groß genug / das man solche seele / die durch die Pawren zu solchem Teuffelichen verbindnis gezwungenn / vnd on jren willen mit jnen so grewlich sůndigen vnd verdampt mův́ssen werden / errettet vnd hůlffe / denn solche seelen seind recht im fegfewr / ia in der hellen vnd Teuffels banden.

---

[93] = NHG 'ihnen'.
[94] ENHG 'bewilligen' = NHG 'einwilligen' / 'übereinstimmen', cf. FWb s.v. 'bewilligen' 3: 'sich dem Willen anderer entsprechend verhalten'.
[95] Probably a term coined by Luther.

Finally, there is one more thing that should rightly concern those in authority, which is that the peasants are not content to belong to the devil themselves, but are urging and forcing many good people, against their will, to join their devilish band, making them share in their wickedness and damnation.[96] For anyone who willingly goes along with them goes to the devil with them as well and is guilty of all the wrongdoing they commit; but such people cannot help it because they have so little faith that they do not put up any resistance. For a good Christian should sooner suffer a hundred deaths than give a hair's breadth of approval to the peasants' cause. Oh, there could now be many martyrs made by the bloodthirsty peasants and prophets of murder![97] But those in authority should have mercy on people who have been taken prisoner by the peasants, and if they had no other reason to feel confident in unleashing the sword against the peasants and risking their own person and property in doing so, it would be more than reason enough to rescue and help such souls, which are forced by the peasants into such a devilish association and compelled against their will to join with them to sin so grievously and to be damned for sure. For these souls are certainly in purgatory;[98] indeed, they are in the bonds of hell and of the devil.

---

[96] Indeed, oaths were sometimes extracted under threat. Doing this, it was thought, would force the swearer to support the movement for fear of the spiritual repercussions of oath breaking, cf. the *Schwarzwälder Artikelbrief* in: *Der deutsche Bauernkrieg, Aktenband* (1935), 346.

[97] Luther's allusion to the prophets of murder should be understood, in part, as a defence against charges that his teachings were responsible for the conflict's outbreak. While he had struck a more purely defensive tone on this point in the *Ermahnung zum Frieden* (cf. chapter 1.1; 3.1), here he went on the attack, accusing more radical reformers – especially Thomas Müntzer (chapter 1.2) – of having riled up the peasantry.

[98] Luther appears to have been finding the doctrine of Purgatory particularly challenging around 1525, mentioning it in several publications. He took pains to stress that he could still not exclude the possibility that it existed, despite it not being mentioned in the Bible, cf. Kim (2025), 58–59. Luther had his final reckoning with the doctrine of Purgatory in *Widerruf vom Fegefeuer* (1530); *WA* 30.2 (1909), 367–90.

Drumb lieben herren[99] loset[100] hie / rettet hie / helfft hie / erbarmet[101] euch der armen leut / Steche / schlahe / würge hie wer da kan / bleybstu drüber todt / wol dir / seliglichern tod kanstu nymmer mehr überkomen / Denn du stirbst in gehorsam Göttlichs wortes vnd befehls / Roma[nos] .xiij.[102] vnnd im dienst der liebe / deinen (a4v) nechsten zuretten auß der hellen vnnd Teuffelsbanden. So bitte ich nun / fliehe von den Pawren wer da kan / als vom Teuffel selbs. Die[103] aber nicht fliehenn / bitte ich Gott wollte sie erleuchten vnd bekeren. Welche aber nicht zubekeren seind da gebe Gott / das sie kein glück noch gelingen haben müssen Hie spreche[104] ein iglicher frommer[105] Christ / Amen.[106] Denn das gebett ist recht vnd gut / vnd gefellet Gott wol / das weyss ich. Dunckt das yemandt zu hart / der denck das vntreglich ist auffrur / vnd alle stunde der wellt verstörung zuwarten sey.

---

[99] Referring to the princes and people in authority.
[100] = NHG 'erlösen'.
[101] The first line of the paragraph (up to *erbarmet*) is underlined, the rest of the paragraph highlighted by a bracket running down on the right-hand side, and next to the first line is the ironic comment *seüberlich* ('neat' or 'tidy') as reaction to this solution strategy.
[102] Romans 13:5: *Wherefore ye must needs be subject, not only for wrath, but also for conscience sake* (KJV). *So seid nu aus not vnterthan / nicht alleine vmb der straffe willen / sondern auch vmb des Gewissens willen* (L45).
[103] = NHG 'diejenigen'.
[104] Optative / third person singular present subjunctive.
[105] ENHG 'frum' in a broader sense, more like MHG 'vrum' (valiant) than NHG 'fromm' (pious).
[106] Luther regularly includes prayer-like sentences ending in 'Amen' in his pamphlets. 'Amen' works here in the sense he explained in his versification of the Lord's Prayer 'Vater unser im Himmelreich': 'Amen, das ist: es werde wahr'.

And so, dear lords, come and redeem, come and rescue, come and help, have mercy on these poor folk! Whoever can do so, come and stab, strike, and strangle! If you die in doing so, good for you: a more blessed death you can never achieve, for you die in obedience to God's word and commandment and to rescue your (a4v) neighbour from the bonds of hell and of the devil in the service of love (Romans 13). So I now implore everyone: flee from the peasants if you can as from the devil himself. But those who do not flee, I pray that God might enlighten and convert them. As for those who will not be converted, God grant that they can find neither fortune nor success. Here let every good Christian say 'Amen'. For this prayer is right and good and well pleasing to God; of this I am certain. If anyone considers this too harsh,[107] let him consider that rebellion is intolerable, and that the destruction of the world can be expected at any moment.

---

[107] Many of Luther's own friends found this pamphlet too harsh, yet he never disavowed it, cf. chapter 1.1. Still, he lamented scarcely a month after its publication "the outrage... that I have caused with the pamphlet against the peasants! Now everything is forgotten which God did in the world through me. Now lords, clergy, peasants, all are against me, and threaten me with death". (*Welch ein Zetergeschrei... hab ich angericht mit dem Büchlin wider die Bauren! Da ist alles vergessen, was Gott der Welt durch mich getan hat. Nun sind Herrn, Pfaffen, Bauren, alles wider mich, und dräuen mir den Tod.*), cf. *WABr* 3, 531, 4-7; Kaufmann (2025), 200.

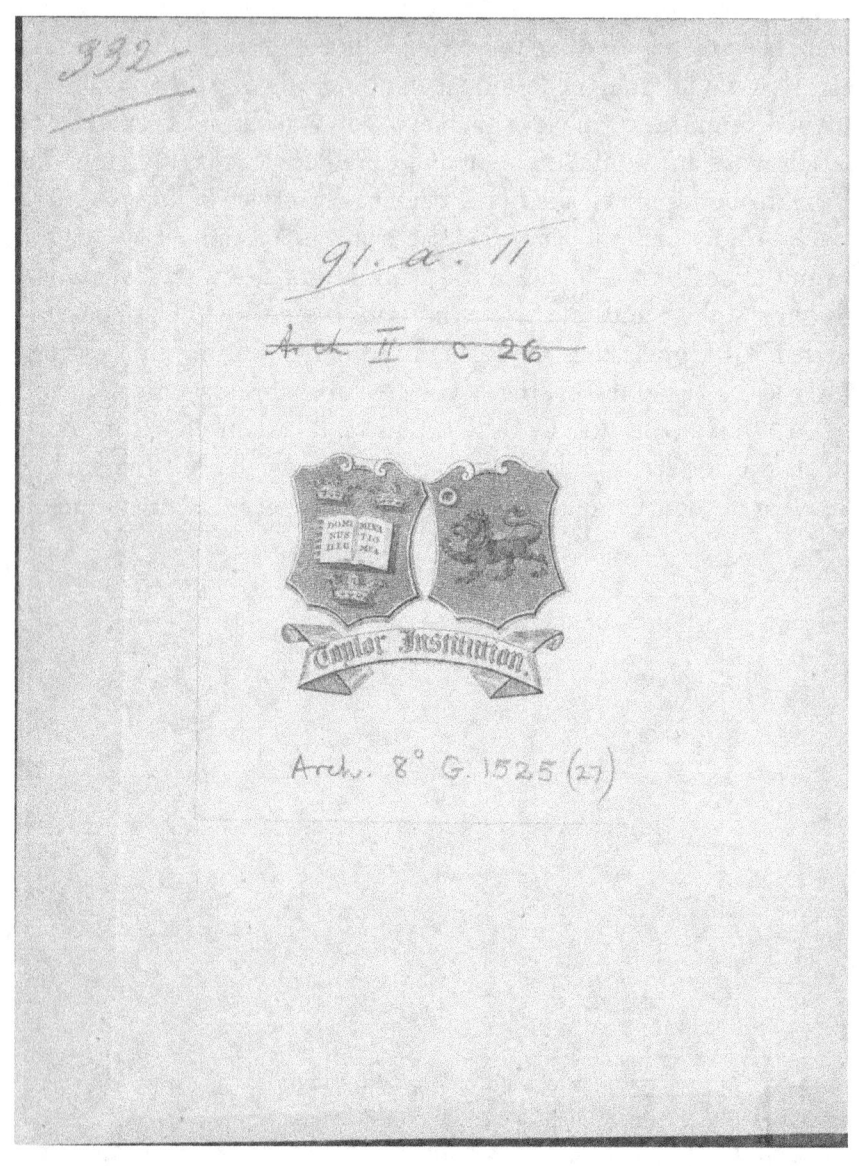

Taylor Institution Library, ARCH.8°.G.1525(27), upper paste-down
The 19th-century library stamp shows the University of Oxford coat of arms and
those of Sir Robert Taylor plus various shelfmarks since its acquisition
see Clare Hills-Nova <u>Unpacking Sir Robert Taylor's Library</u> (19/12/2014)

Facsimile

The two facsimiles have been placed on facing pages to be able to tell the different approach of Friedrich Peypus in the Nuremberg edition (left = the basis for the edition) and Matthäus Maler in the Erfurt edition (right).
The pages have been slightly downsized to three quarters (14.5 × 11cm) of the original quarto format which is roughly equivalent to A5 (19 × 12.5cm).

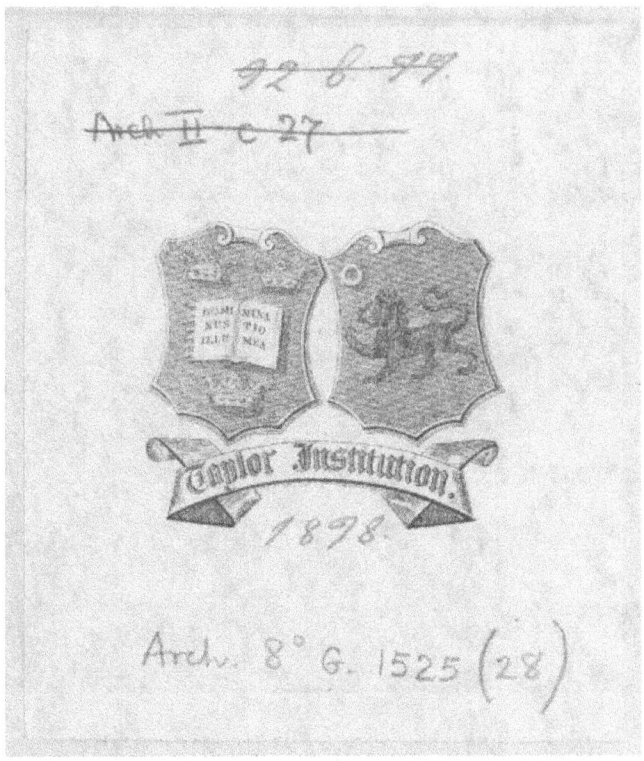

Taylor Institution Library, ARCH.8°.G.1525(28), book plate on upper paste-down
The date '1878' shows that the Erfurt edition was acquired in the same year as the batch of Reformation pamphlets from Heidelberg to which the Nuremberg edition belonged

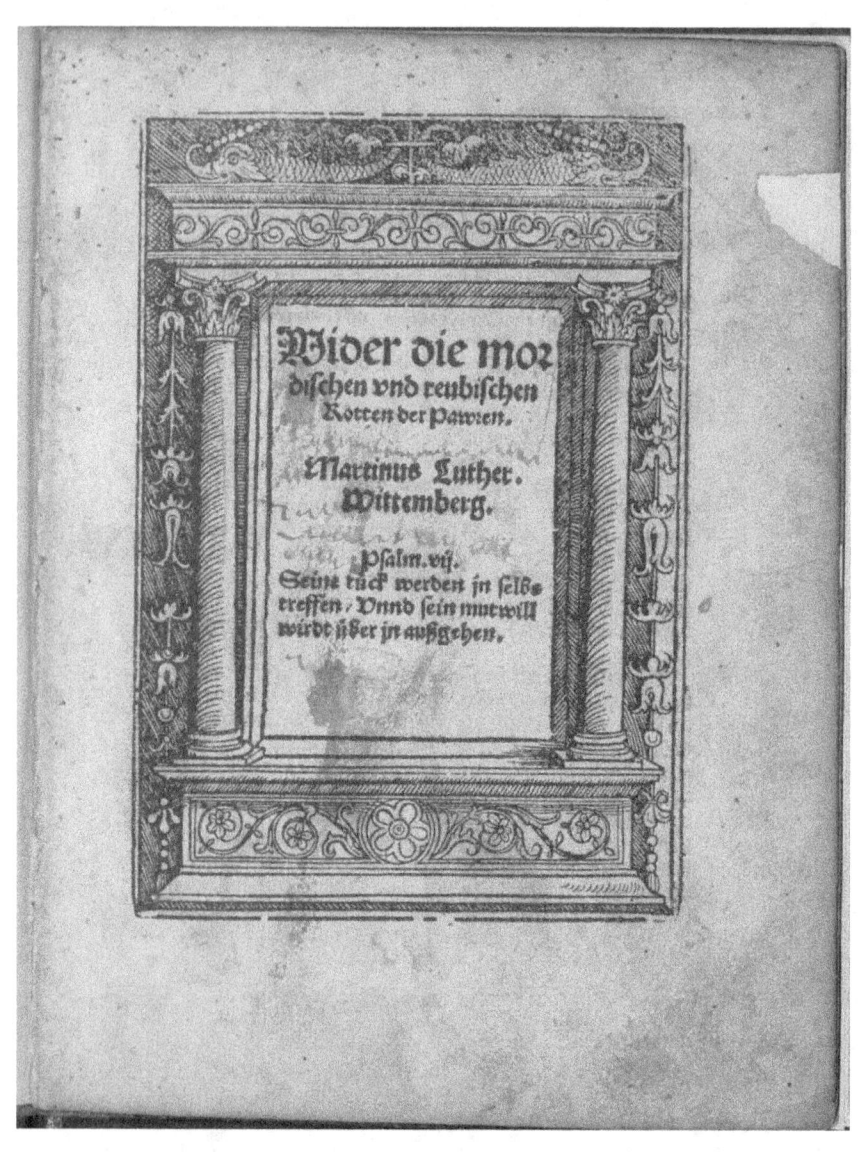

Taylor Institution Library, ARCH.8°.G.1525(27), a1r
Titlepage with pen trials by an early reader, see chapter 3.1

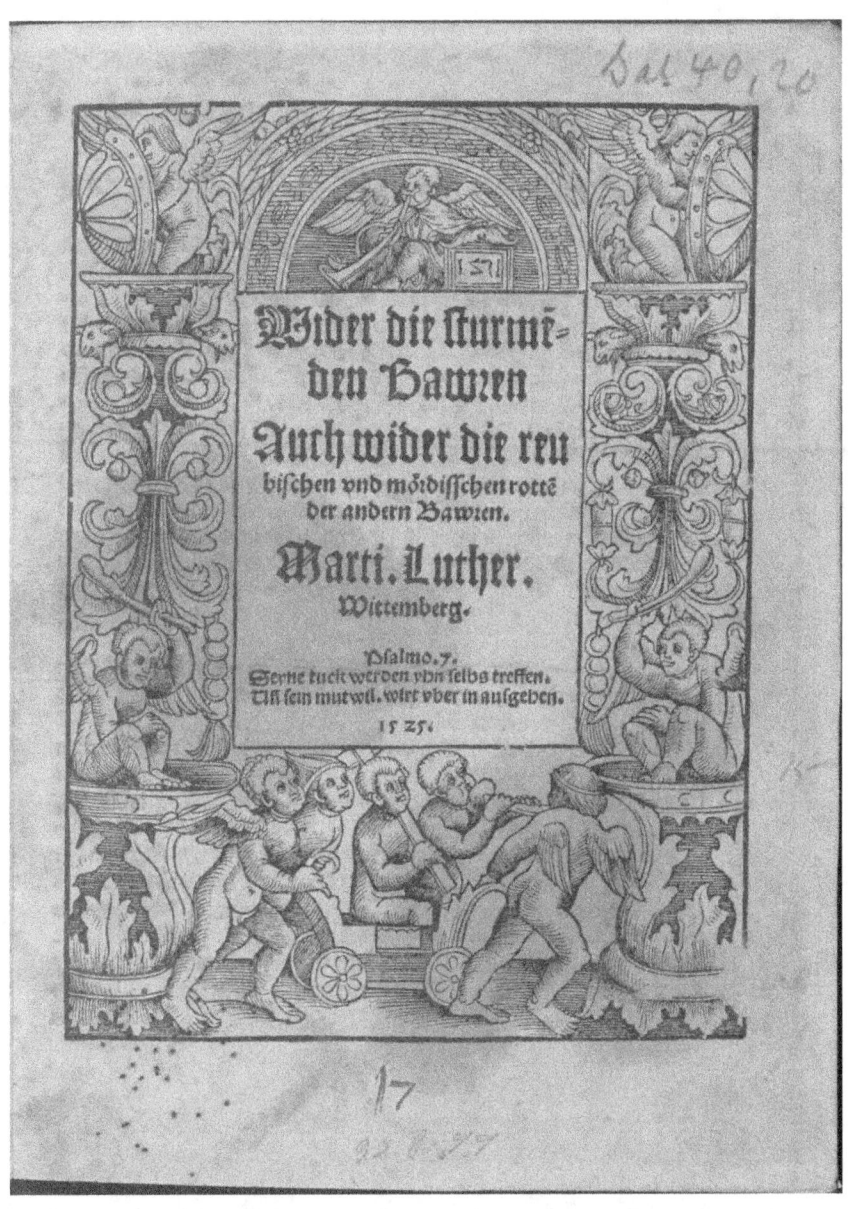

Taylor Institution Library, ARCH.8°.G.1525(28), a1r
Title woodcut with the mirrored 1521 dating, see chapter 3.2.
The pencil marking 'Sal' indicates that it came from the library of Kloster Salem

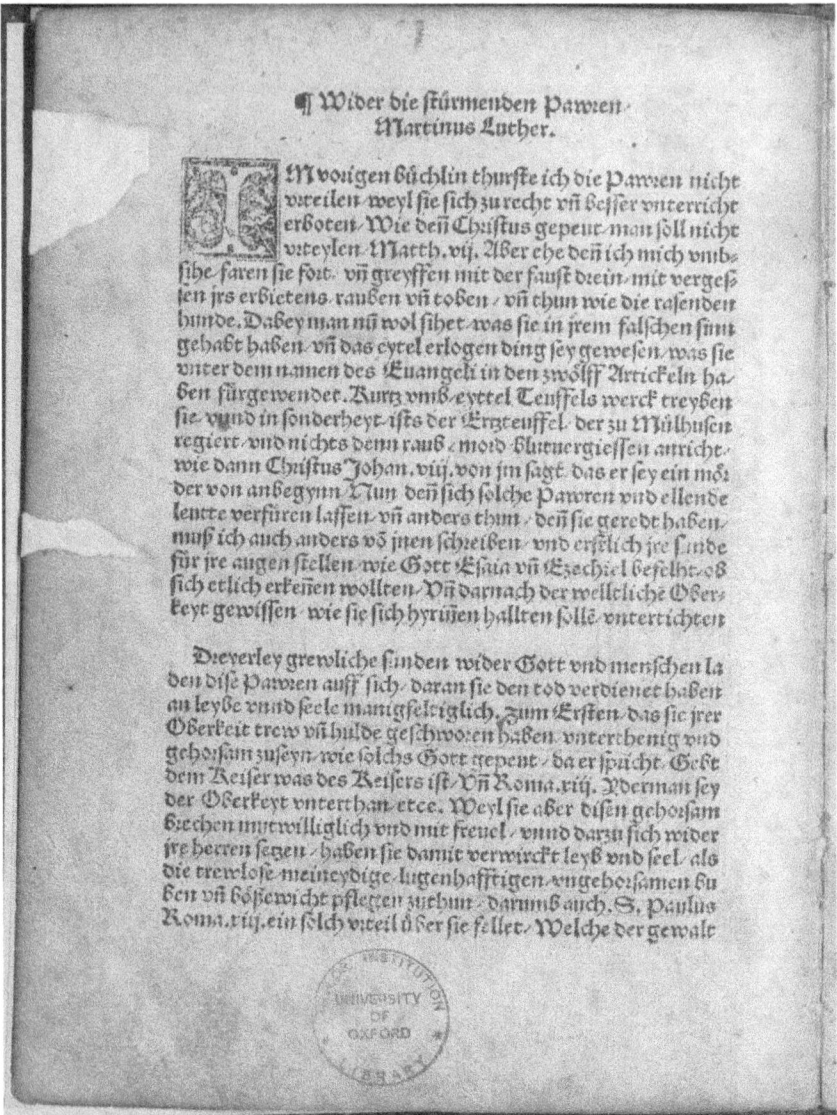

Taylor Institution Library, ARCH.8°.G.1525(27), a1v
The tear at the side points to the removal of a tab which would have marked the position in a *Sammelband* of pamphlets

¶ Widder die Stürmenden Bawren
Martinus Luther.

JM vörigen büchlin thürste ich dy Bawren nicht vrteyle/ weil sie sich zu recht vnnd besser vnterricht erbotten/ wie denn Christus gepeut/ man solle nicht vrteylen Math. 7. Aber ehe denn ich mich vmbsihe/ faren sie furt/ vnnd greyffen mit der faust dreyn/ mitt vergessen yhres erbietens/ rauben vnd toben/ vnnd thun wie die rasenden hunde. Dabey man nu wol sihet/ was sie ynn yhrem falschenn synn gehabt haben/ vnnd das eyttell erlogen ding sey gewesen/ was sie vnter dem namen des Euangeli ynn den zwelff artickeln haben furgewendett Kurtz vmb/ eyttel teuffels werck treybenn sie/ Vnnd ynn sunderheydt ists der Ertzteuffell/ der zcu Mülhausenn regirt/ vnd nichts denn raub/ mordt/ blutvergiessenn anrichtt/ wye denn Christus Johan. 8. von yhm sagt/ das er sey eyn mörder von anbegyn. Nu denn sich solche bawren vnnd elende leute verfuren lassen/ vnnd anders thun/ denn sie geredt haben/ mus ich auch anders vonn yhnen schreyben/ vnnd erstlich yhre sünde fur yhre augen stellen/ wie Gott Esaia vnd Ezechiel befelht/ ob sich etlich erkennen wolten/ Vnnd darnach der weltlichenn öberkeyt gewissenn/ wie sie sich hier ynnen halten sollen/ vnterrichten.

¶ Dreyerley grewliche sünden widder Got vnnd menschen laden diese bawren auff sich/ daran sie den todt verdienet haben/ ann leyb vnd seele manichfaltiglich.

Zum ersten/ das sie yhur öberkeyt trew vnnd hulde geschworen haben/ vntterthenig vnd gehorsam zu seyn/ wie solchs Got gepeut/ da er spricht. Gebt dem keyser/ was des keysers ist. Vnnd Ro. 13. Jderman sey der öberkeyt vnterthan rc. Weyl sie aber disenn gehorsam brechen mutwilliglich vnnd mitt freuel/ vnnd dazu sich widder yhre herrenn setzen/ habenn sie damit verwirckt leyb vnnd seel/ alls die trewlose/ meyneydige/lügenhafftigenn/ vngehorsamenn buben vnnd bösewicht pflegen zuthun/ darumb auch S. Paulus Ro. 13. eyn solch vrteyl vber sie fellet. Welche der gewallt widderstrebenn/ die werden eyn gericht vber sich vberkomen/ Welcher spruch auch die Bawren

Taylor Institution Library, ARCH.8°.G.1525(28), a1v
The University Library of Heidelberg marked it as duplicate with a 'duplum' stamp, the Taylor Institution library bought it in the 19th century on the suggestion of Friedrich Max Müller and stamped it in the 20th century.

widerstreben die werdenn ein gericht über sich überkomen. Welcher spruch auch die Pawren entlich treffen wirdt, es ge schehe kurtz oder lange, denn Gott will trew vnd pflicht ge hallten haßen.

Zum Andern, das sie Auffrur anrichten, rauben vnd plun dern mit freuel Clöster vnnd Schlösser, die nicht jr seind, da mit sie als die offenlichen strassenreuber vnd mörder, alleine wol zwiffeltig den tod an leyb vnnd seele verschulden. Auch ein auffrürischer mensch, den man des bezeugen kan, schon ist Gottes vnnd Keyserlicher Acht ist, das wer am ersten kan vnnd mag denselben erwürgen recht vn wol thut. Den über einen offenlichen auffrürgen, ist ein iglicher mensch, beyde oberrichter vnd scharffrichter, gleych als wenn ein fewr an gehet, wer am ersten kan lesschen, der ist der beste, denn Auff rur ist nicht ein schlechter mord, sondern wie ein groß fewr das ein land anzündet vn verwustet, also bringt Auffrur mit sich ein land vol mords, blutvergissen, vnnd mache widwyn vnd waisen, vn verstöret alles, wie das allergrössest vnglück Drumb sol hie zuschmeissen, würgen vnd stechen, heymlich oder offenlich, wer da kan, vn gedencke das nicht gifftigers *gemachh* schedlichers, teuffelischers seyn kan, denn ein auffrürischer mensch, gleich als wenn man einen tollen hund todschlahen muß, schlegstu nit, so schlegt er dich vn ein gantz land mit dir

Zum Dritten, das sie solche schreckliche, grewlicke sünde mit dem Euangelio decken, nennen sich Christliche brüder nemen eyd vnd hulde, vn zwingen die leutte zu solchen grew eln, mit jnen zuhallten, damit sie die allergrösten Gottsleste rer vn schender seines heyligen namens werden vn ehren vn dienen also dem Teuffel vnter dem scheyn des Euangelii, dar an sie wol zehen mal den tod verdienen an leyb vnd seele, das ich heßlicher sünde nie gehört habe. Vnd achte auch, das der Teuffel den iüngsten tag süle, das er solch vnerhörte stück für nimpt, als solt er sagenn, Es ist das letzte, drumb solt es das

A ij

die Bawren endtlich treffain wirdt/ es geschehe kurtz obber lange/ den Got will trew vnd pflicht gehalten haben.

Zum andern/ das sie auffrur anrichten/ rauben vnnd plundern mitt freuell clöster vnnd schlösser/ die nicht yhr sindt/ damit sie/ alls die offentlichen strassen reuber vnnd morder/ alleyne woll zweyfeltig den todt an leyb vn̄ seele verschulden. Auch eyn auffrürischer mensch den mann des bezeugen kann/ schonn in Gottes vnnd Keyserlicher acht ist/ das/ wer am ersten kann vnnd mag/ den selben erwurgen/ recht vnd woll thut. Denn vber eynen offentlichen auffrürigen/ ist eyn yglicher mensch beyde vber richter vnnd scharpffrichter/ gleych alls wenn eyn fewr angehet/ wer am ersten kann leschenn/ der ist der best/ denn auffrur ist nicht eynn schlechter mordt/ sondern wie eynn gross fewr/ das eyn landt anzundet vnd verwüstet/ also bringt auff rur mit sich eyn landt vol mords/ blutuergiessen/ vnnd macht wid/ wen vnd weysen/ vnd verstöret alles/ wie das aller grössest vnglück Drumb soll hye zu schmeyssen/ wurgen vnd stechen/ heymlich oder offenlich/ wer da kan/ vnd gedencken/ das nichts gyfftigers/ sched/ lichers/ teuffdischers seynn kann/ denn eynn auffrürischer mensch/ gleych alls wen man eynen tollen hundt todtschlahen muß/ schlegstu nicht/ so schlegt er dich/ vnd eyn gantz landt mit dyr.

Zum dritten/ das sie solche schreckliche/ grewliche sünde/ mitt dem Euangelion decken/ nennen sich Christliche bruder/ nemen eyd vnd hulde/ vnnd zwingen die laute zu solchen greweln/ mit yhnenn zu halten/ damit sie die aller grössenn Gots lesterer/ vnnd schender seynes heyligen namenn werden/ vnnd ehren vnnd dienen also dem teuffel/ vnter dem scheyn des Ewangelij/ daran sie wol zehen mall den todt verdienen an leyb vnd seele/ das ich heyfflicher sünde nie ge hört habe. Vnnd achte auch/ das der teuffel denn jüngsten tag füle das er solch vnterhörte stück furnympt/ als solt er sagen. Es ist das letzte/ drumb soll es das ergste seynn/ vnnd will die grundtsuppe rü ren vnnd den boden gar auffstossen/ Got wölle yn weren. Da sihe/ welch eynn mechtiger furst der teuffell ist/ Wie er die welet ynn henden hat/ vnnd in eyn annder mangen kann/ Der so baldt so viell tausent Bawren/ fangenn/ verfuren/ verblenden/ verstocken vnnd

ij

ergste seyn/ vñ will die grundsuppen rüren/vñ den poden gar aufstoffen. Gott wöll jn weren. Da sihe welch ein mechtiger Fürst der Teuffel ist/ wie er die wellt in henden hat/ vnd ineinander mengen kan/ der so pald so vil tausent pawren/ fangen/ verfüren/ verblenden/ verstocken/ vnd empören kan/ vñ mit jn machen was sein aller wütigister grym fürnimpt.

Es hilfft auch die pawren nicht das sie fürgeßen/ Gen.j. vnd.ij. Es seyen alle ding frey vnd gemeyne geschaffen/ vnd das wir alle gleych getaufft seind. Deñ im newen Testamēt hellt vnd gillt Moses nicht/ sondern da stehet vnser meister Christus/ vñ wüfft vns mit leyb vñ gut vnter den Keiser vñ welltlich recht/ da er spricht/ Gebt dem Keiser was des Keisers ist. So spricht auch paulus Roma.xij. zu allen getaufftē Christen/ Yderman sey der gewallt vntertthan. Vnd petrus/ Seyt vntertthan aller menschlicher ordnüg. Diser lere Christi seind wir schuldig zugeleben/ wie der vatter vom hymel geseut vnnd sagt/ Dis ist mein lieber Sün/ den höret. Deñ die tauffe macht nicht leyb vñ gut frey/ sondern die seelen. Auch macht das Euangelion nicht die güter gemeyn/ on alleine welche solchs williglich von jn selbs thun wölle/ wie die Aposteln vñ jünger/ Act.iiij.thetten/ welche nicht die frembden güter pilati vñ Herodis gemeyn zuseyn fodderten/ wie vnser vnsinige paurn toben/ sonder jr eygen güter. Aber vnser pawren wöllē der andern frembden güter gemein habē vñ jr eygē für sich behallten. Das seind mir feine Christē/ Jch meyn das kein Teuffel mehr in der helle sey/ sonder allzumal in die pawren seind gefarē. Es ist überauß vñ über alle masse das wütē.

Weyl deñ nun die pawren auff sich laden/ beyde Gott vñ menschen/ vñ so manigfelltiglich schon des tods an leyb vnd seel schuldig seind/ vnd keins rechten gestehen noch warten/ sondern ymer fort toben/ muß ich hie die welltliche Oberkeyt vnterrichten/ wie sie hierinne mit gutem gewissen faren solle. Erstlich der Oberkeyt/ so da kan vñ will/ on vorgehe.id erbie=

empören kann/ vnnd mit yhnn machen was seyn aller wütigester grym furnympt.

Es hylfft auch die Bawren nicht/ das sie furgeben Genesis.1. vnd 2. seyen alle ding frey vnd gemeyne geschaffen/ vnd das wir alle gleych getaufft sindt. Denn im newenn Testament helle vnnd gylle Moses nicht/ sondern da stehet vnser meyster Christus/ vnd wurfft vns mit leyb vnd gut vndter den Keyser vnnd weltlich recht/ da er spricht. Gebt dem Keyser/ was des Keysers ist. So spricht auch Paulus Ro.13. zu allen getaufften christen. yderman sey der gewalt vndterthan. Vnnd Petrus. Seyt vndterthan allen menschlichenn ordnung. Dieser lere Christi sind wir schuldig zu geleben/ wie der vater vom hymell gebeut vnd sagt. Dyß ist mein lieber son/ den höret. Denn die tauffe macht nicht leyb vnnd gut frey/ sondern die seelen. Auch macht das Euangelion nicht die gütter gemeyn/ on alleyne/ wilche solchs williglich von yhn selbs thun wöllen/ wie die Aposteln vnd Jünger Act. 4. thetten/ wilche nicht die fremdden gütther Pilatis vnd Herodis gemeyn zu seyn fodderten/ wie vnser vnsinnige Bawren toben/ sonder yhr eygen gütther. Aber vnser Bawren wöllen der andern fremdden gütther gemeyn haben/ vnd yhr eygen fur sich behalten. Das sind mir feyne Christen/ Jch meyn das keyn teuffell mehr in der helle sey/ sondern alzumall in die Bawren sind gefaren. Es ist vber auß vnnd vber alle masse/ das wüten.

Weyll den nhu die Bawren auff sich laden/ beyde Gott vnnd menschen/ vnd so mancherleytiglich schon des tods an leyb vnd seele schuldig sind/ vnnd keyns rechten gestehen noch warten/ sondern ymer fort toben/ muß ich hye die weltliche oberkeyt vndterrichtenn/ wie sie hyryn mit gutem gewissen faren sollen. Erstlich der oberkeyt so da kan vnd wil/ on vorgehend erbieten zum recht vnd billigkeyt/ solche Bawren schlahen vnnd straffen/ will ich nicht weren/ ob sie gleych das Euangelion nicht leydet/ denn sie hatt des guth recht/ Sintemall die Bawren nn nicht mehr vmb das Euangelion fechtenn/ sondernn sind offentlich wordenn/ trewlose/ meyneydige/ vngehorsame/ auffrurische/ mörder/ rewber/ gottslesterer/ wilche auch Heydnische oberkeyt zu straffen recht vnnd macht hat/ ia da zu schuldig.

ten zum recht vñ billigkeyt/solche Pawren schlahen vñ straf-
fen/will ich nicht wehren/ob sie gleych das Euangelion mit
leydet/Deñ sie hat des gut recht/Sintemal die Pawren nun
nicht mehr vmb das Euangelion fechten/sonder seind offentlich worden trewlose/meyneydige/vngehorsame/auffrürische/
mörder/reuber/gottslesterer/welche auch heydenische Oberkeyt zustraffen recht vñ macht hat/ia dazu schuldig ist/solche
buben zustraffen.Denn darumb tregt sie das schwert/vnd ist
Gottes dienerin über den so übels thut. Roma.xiij.

Aber die Oberkeyt so Christlich ist vñ das Euangelion ley-
det/derhalbenn auch die Pawren keinen scheyn wider sie haben soll hie mit forcht handeln. Vnnd zum ersten die sachen
Gott heymgeben/vñ bekennen/das wir solchs wol verdient
haben.Dazu sorgen/das Gott villeicht den Teuffel also errege zu gemeyner straffe Teutschs lannds. Darnach demütig-
lich bitten wider den Teuffel vmb hülffe/Denn wir fechten
hie nicht alleine wider blut vnnd fleysch/sondern wider die
geystlichen böse wicht in der lufft/welche mit gebert müssen
angegriffen werden. Weñ nun das hertze so gegen Gott gerichtet ist/das man seinen göttlichen willen lest wallten/ob
er vns wölle oder nicht wölle zu Fürsten vñ herren haben/soll
man sich gegen die tollen Pawrē zum überfluß(ob sie es wol
nicht werdt seind)zu recht vnd gleychem erbieten . Darnach
wo das nicht helffen will/flucks zum schwert greyffen.

Denn ein Fürst vnd Herr muß hie dencken wie er Gottes
amptman vnnd seins zorns diener ist Romano.xiij. dem das
schwert über solche buben befolhen ist/Vnd sich eben so hoch
für Gott versündigt/wo er nicht strafft vñ wehret/vnd sein
ampt nicht volfüret/als weñ einer mördet/dem das schwert
nicht befolhen ist.Deñ wo er kan vñ strafft nicht/es sey durch
mord oder blutuergiessen/so ist er schuldig an allem mord vnd
übel/das solche buben begebē/als der da mutwilliglich durch
nachlassen seins göttlichen befelhs zulest solche boßheyt zu-

A iij

zu schůldig ist/ solche buben zu straffen/ Denn darumb tregt sie das schwerdt/ vnd ist Gots dieneryn vber den so vbels thut. Rom.13.

Aber die oberkeyt/ so Christlich ist/ vnnd das Euangelion ley= det/ der halben auch die Bawren keynen scheynn widder sie haben/ soll hye mit furchten handeln. Vnd zum ersten die sachen got heym geben/ vnnd bekennen/ das wir solchs woll virdienet haben. Darzu besorgen/ das Gott vielleicht denn teuffell also ergere/ zcu gemeyner straffe Deutsch landts. Darnach demůttigklich bitten widder denn teuffell vmb hůlffe. Den wir feehten hye nicht alleyne widder bluth vnnd fleysch/ sondern widder die geystlichen böswicht in der lufft/ wilche mit gebeth mussen angriffen werden. Wenn nhu das hertze so gegenn Gott gericht ist/ das man seynen Götlichen willenn lest walten/ ob er vnns wölle odder nicht wölle zu Fursten vnnd Herren haben/ soll man sich gegen die tolle Bawren czum vberfluß (ob sie es woll nicht werdt sindt) zu recht vnd gleychem erbieten. Darnach wo das nicht helffen will/ flur zum schwerdt greyffen.

Den eyn Furst vnd Herr muß hye dencken/ wie er Gottes ampt man vnnd seyns zorns diener ist. Rom. 13. dem das schwerdt vber solche buben befolhen ist. Vnd sich eben so hoch fur got versundige wo er nicht strafft vnnd weret/ vnd sein ampt nicht volfůret/ alls wen eyner mordet/ dem das schwerdt nicht befolhen ist. Denn wo er kan/ vnnd strafft nicht/ es sey durch mordt odder blutvergiessen/ so ist er schuldig an allem mordt vnnd vbell/ das solche buben bege= henn/ alls der da mutwilligklich durch nachlassen seyns Gotlichen befelhs/ zuleßt/ solchenn buben yhre boßheyt zu vbenn/ so erß woll weren kan vnnd schuldig ist/ darumb ist hye nicht zu schlaffen. Es gylle auch hye nicht gedult odder barmhertzigkeydt. Es ist des sch= werdts vnd zorns zeyt hye/ vnd nicht der gnaden zeyt.

<u>So soll nu die oberkeyt hye getrost fort dringen/ vnd mit guttem gewissen dreyn schlahenn/ weyll sie eyne ader regen kann. Denn hye ist das vorteyl/ das die Bawren böse gewissen vnd vnrechte sachen haben/ vnd wilcher Bawr daruber erschlagen wird/ mit leyb vnd seele verlorn/ vnd ewig des teuffells ist. Aber die oberkeyt hat eyn gut gewissen vnnd rechte sachen/ vnnd kan zu Gott also sagen mit aller sicherheyt</u>

üben/ so ers wol wehren kan vnd schuldig ist. Darumb ist hie nicht zuschlaffen. Es gillt auch nicht hie gedult oder barmhertzigkeyt. Es ist des schwerts vnd zorns zeyt hie, vnd nicht der genaden zeyt.

So soll nun die Oberkeyt hie getrost fort tringen, vnd mit gutem gewissen dreyn schlahen, weyl sie eine ader regen kan, denn hie ist das vortail, das die Pawren böse gewissen vnnd vnrechte sachen haben vn welcher Pawr darüber erschlagen wirdt, mit leyb vnd seel verloren vnnd ewig des Teuffels ist. Aber die Oberkeyt hat ein gut gewissen vnnd rechte sachen, vnd kan zu Gott also sagen, mit aller sicherheyt des hertzen, Sihe mein Gott du hast mich zum Fürsten oder herre gesetzt daran ich nicht kan zweyffeln, vnd hast mir das schwert befolhen über die übelthetter, Rom. xiij. Es ist dein wort vn mag nicht liegen, So muß ich solch ampt bey verlust deiner gnaden außrichten, So ists auch offentlich, das dise Pawren vilfaltig vor dir vnd vor der welle den tod verdienet, vnd mir zu straffen befolhen. Willen nun mich durch sie lassen tödten, vnd mir die Oberkeyt wider nemen vnd vntergehen lassen, wolan, so geschehe dein wille. So sterbe ich doch vnnd gehe vnter in deinem Göttlichen besehl vnd wort, vn werd erfunden im gehorsam deines besehls vnd meines ampts. Drumb will ich straffen vn schlahen so lange ich eine ader regen kan, du wirsts wol richten vnd machen.

Also kans denn geschehen, das wer auff der Oberkeyt seyten erschlagen wirdt, ein rechter merterer vor Gott sey, so er mit solchem gewissen streyt, wie gesagt ist. Denn er gehet in Göttlichem wort vnnd gehorsam. Widerumb was auff der Pawren seyten vmbkompt, ein ewiger hellebrandt ist, den er füret das schwert wider Gottes wort vnd gehorsam, vnd ist ein Teuffels glied. Vn obs gleych geschehe das die Pawren oblegen, da Gott für sey, den Gott seind alle ding müglich, vn wir nicht wissen, ob er villeicht zu vorlauffst des jüngsten

ſicherheyt des hertzen. Syhe/ mein Got/ du haſt mich zum Furſten oder Herren geſetzt/ daran ich nicht kan zweyffeln. Vnnd haſt mir das ſchwerd befolhen vber die vbeltheter. Ro.13. Es iſt dein wordt vnnd mag nicht liegen/ ſo muß ich ſolchs ampt/ bey verluſt deiner gnaden/ außrichten/ ſo iſts auch offentlich/ das dieſe Bawren vielfaltig fur dir vnd der welt den todt verdienet/ vnnd mir zu ſtraffen befolhen. Wileu nu mich durch ſie laſſen tödten/ vnd mir die oberkeyt widernemen vnd vndergehen laſſen/ Wolan/ ſo geſchehe dein wille/ So ſterbe ich doch vnd gehe vnter in deynem götlichen befelh vnd wordt/ vnnd werd erfunden im gehorſam deines befelhs vnnd meynes ampts. Drumb will ich ſtraffen/ vnd ſchlahen ſo lange ich eyne ader regen kan. Du wirſts woll richten vnd machen.

Alſo kauß dem geſchehen/ das/ wer auff der oberkeyt ſeytten erſchlagen wirdt/ eyn rechter marterer fur Got ſey/ ſo er mit ſolchem gewiſſen ſtreydt/ wie geſagt iſt. Denn er geht ym Götlichenn wordt vnd gehorſam. Widderumb/ was auff der Bawren ſeytten vmb kompt/ eyn ewiger hellebrand iſt. Denn er furet das ſchwerdt widder gotes wordt vnd gehorſam/ vnd iſt ein teuffels gleyd/ Vnnd obs gleych geſchehe/ das die Bawren obligenn (da Got fur ſey) Denn Got ſind alle ding müglich/ vnnd wir nicht wiſſen/ ob er vielleycht zum vorlaufft des iüngſtenn tags/ welcher nicht ferne ſeynn will/ wölle durch denn teuffell alle ordnung vnnd oberkeyt zuſtören vnnd die welle in eynen wüſten hauffen werffen. So ſterbenn doch ſicher vnnd gehenn zcu ſcheyternn mitt gutthem gewiſſenn/ die in yhrem ſchwerdt ampt funden werden/ vnd laſſen dem teuffell das weltlich reych/ vnnd nehmenn dafur das ewig reych. Solch wunderliche zeyten ſind ytzt/ das eyn Furſt den hymell mit blutvergieſſen verdienen kan/ baß dan andere mit betthen.

Am ende iſt noch eyne ſache/ die billich ſoll die oberkeyt bewegen Denn die Bawren laſſen yhnn nicht benügenn/ das ſie des teuffells ſindt/ ſondern zwingenn vnnd dringenn viel frummer leuthe/ die es vngerne thunn/ zu yrem teuffeliſchen bunde/ vnnd machenn die ſelbigen alſo teylhafftig aller yhrer boßheyt vnd verdambnuß/ Denn wer mit yhnn bewilliget/ der fert auch mit yhnn zum teuffell/ vnnd iſt ſchuldig

Taylor Institution Library, ARCH.8°.G.1525(28), a3v
A contemporary reader marked the passage that it is easier for prince to go to heaven via violence than prayer with *NB* (*nota bene*) in the margin.

tags (welcher nicht ferne seyn will) wölle durch den Teuffel
alle ordnung vnd oberkeyt zůstören, vnnd die wellt in einen
wüsten hauffen werffen. So sterben doch sicher vnnd gehen
zuscheyttern mit gutem gewissen, die in jrem schwertampt
funden werden, vnd lassen dem Teuffel das welltlich reich,
vn nemen dafür das ewige reich. Solch wunderliche zeyten
seind itzt, das ein Fürst den hymel mit plutvergiessen verdie
nen kan, baß, denn andere mit betten.

Am ende ist noch ein sache, die billich soll die Oberkeyt be=
wegen. Denn die Pawren lassen jn nicht benügen, das sie des
Teuffels seind, sondern zwingen vnd dringen vil fromer leu=
te die es vngerne thun zu jrem Teuffelischen bunde, vn mach
en dieselbigen also teylhafftig aller jrer boßheyt vn verdam=
nis. Denn wer mit jn bewilliget, der fert auch mit jn zum Teu
fel vn ist schuldig aller übelthat die sie begehen, vn müssens
doch thun, weyl sie so schwachs glaubens seind, das sie nicht
widersteben. Denn hundert tödte solt ein frommer Christ ley=
den, ehe er ein harbreit in der Pawren sache bewilliget. O vil
merterer kundten itzt werden durch die plutdürstigen Paw=
ren vnd mordpropheten. Nun solcher gefangener vnter den
Pawren sollten sich die Oberkeyt erbarmen, vn wenn sie sonst
keine sache hetten, das schwert getröst wider die Pawren ge
hen zulassen, vn selbs leyb vnd gut dran zusetzen, so were doch
dise überig groß genug, das man solche seele, die durch die
Pawren zu solchem Teuffelischen verbindnis gezwungem=
vn on jren willen mit jnen so grewlich sündige vn verdampt
müssen werden, errettet vnd hülffe, denn solche seelen seind
recht im Fegfewr, ia in der hellen vnd Teuffels banden.

Darumb liebe herrn loset hie, rettet hie, helfft hie, erbarmet
euch der armen leut. Steche, schlahe, würge hie wer da kan,
bleybstu drüber todt, wol dir, schiglichern tod kanstu nymmer
meht überkomen. Denn du stirbst in gehorsam Göttlichs wor=
tes vnd befelhs, Rom. xiij. vnnd im dienst der liebe, deinen

ist schäbig aller vbelthat/ die sie begehen/ vnnd muessens doch thun
weyll sie so schwachs glaubens sind/ das sie nicht widderstehenn/
Denn hundert tödte solt eynn fromer Christ leyden/ ehe er eynn har
breyt ynn der Bawrenn sache bewilliget. O viell merterer kundtenn
itzt werden durch die blutdurstigen Bawren vnnd mordtpropheten
Nu solcher gefangener vnter denn Bawren solten sich die oberkeyt
erbarmen. Vnnd wen sie sonst keyne sache hetten/ das schwerd wi=
der die Bawren getrost gehen zcu lassen/ vnnd selbs leyb vnnd gutt
dran zu setzen/ so were doch diese vberig gros gnug/ das man solche
seele/ die durch die Bawrenn zu sollichem teuffellischenn verbundnis
gezwungen/ vnd on yhren willen/ mit yhnen so grewlich sundigen
vnd verdampt mussen werden/ errettet vnd hulff/ den solche seelen
sind recht ym fegfewr/ ya ynn der hellen vnd teuffels banden

Drumb lieben Herrenn löset hye/ rettet hye/ helfft hye/ Erbarmet
euch der armen leuthe/ Steche/ schlahe/ wurge/ hye wer da kann
bleybstu drüber todt/ woll dir/ seliglicherrn todt kanstu nymermehr
vberkommen. Denn du stirbst ynn gehorsam götlichs worts vnd be=
selbs Ro. am. 13. vnd ym dyenst der liebe deynen nehisten zuerretten
aus der hellen vnd teuffels banden/ So bitte ich nu/ flihe von denn
Bawren wer da kan/ als vom teuffel selbs. Die aber nicht flihenn
bitt ich/ Gott wolte sie erleuchten vnd bek ren. Welche aber nicht
zu bekeren sind/ da gebe Got/ das sie kein gluck noch gelingen haben
mussen. Hye sprechen eyn yglicher frummer Christ Amen. Denn das
gepett ist recht vnnd gutt/ vnnd gefellet Gott woll/ das weyß ich.
Duncke das yemandt zu hardt/ der dencke/ das vntreglich ist auff=
ruhr/ vnd alle stunde der welt verstörung zu warten sey.

nechsten zwetten auß der hellen vnnd Teuffels banden. So bitte ich inn/ fliehe von den Päwien wer da kan/ als vom Teuffel selbs. Die aber nicht fliehenn bitte ich Gott wollte sie erleuchten vn bekeren. Welche aber nicht zubekeren seind da gebe Gott/ das sie kein glück noch gelingen haben müssen Hie spreche ein iglicher frommer Christ. Amen. Denn das gebett ist recht vnd gut/ vnd gefellet Gott wol das weyß ich. Dunckt das yemandt zu hart/ der denck das vntreglich ist auffrur/vnd alle stunde der welt verstösung zuwarten sey.

Taylor Institution Library, ARCH.8°.G.1525(28), a4v
The creases and the tear in the centre indicate that the pamphlet was carried around folded before it was put into a *Sammelband* of pamphlets by the Cistercian monks of Salem; on the middle left the shadow of a tab is still visible.

www.ingramcontent.com/pod-product-compliance
Lightning Source LLC
Chambersburg PA
CBHW052054070526
44584CB00017B/2167